A TRIP TO ROME

NCQ TITLES

Legal Fictions	Time Pieces
Politics & Letters	Critical Paranoia
On Yeats: Upon a House	On Joyce: 3 easy essays
Drama & Democracy	On Eliot
Locating Theology	Literary Conversions

Film-texts

A Trip to Rome	A Week in Venice
A Short Break in Budapest	Four Days in Athens
Magic in Prague	The Last Priest of Horus

WWW: the weekend that warped the world

Play texts

Darwin: an evolutionary entertainment
Strange Meetings & Shorts

Eliotics

In preparation

Rubbishing Hockney & other reviews
On Collecting Walter Benjamin
Autobiography & Class Consciousness
Considering Canterbury Cathedral

*Though each can be read independently,
these NCQ publications, taken together,
comprise a single hyper-text collection.*

A TRIP TO ROME

a film-text

Bernard Sharratt

New Crisis Quarterly
2015

NEW CRISIS QUARTERLY

ncq@newcrisisquarterly.myzen.co.uk

First published 2015

ISBN : 978-1-910956-15-1

For
Alan Wall
in homage
&
in memory of
a long friendship

This film-text is not written with actual film production in mind. Though it plays with a variety of film genres, it is primarily intended to be read—and imagined.

Rome is an appropriate place as the setting for my characters and my themes, and the script is designed to be easily supplemented by on-line images and maps of the specified sites and scenes. Other film-texts in this 'city' series are set in Athens, Budapest, Prague, and Venice, and the series will probably conclude with *A Last Sight of Europe*.

The dedication records a general and specific indebtedness, and you are warmly urged to read the brilliant novel, *Badmouth*, by Alan Wall to which this text is, in part, a playful response, and for which I hope he will forgive me.

A film-text is a particularly suitable form for the New Crisis Quarterly imprint, since that name revives the title of a very short-lived periodical whose first, only, and final issue appeared in 1984, under the guise of my *The Literary Labyrinth*. Its editorial programme was to publish reviews of imagined books I didn't feel I had the time actually to write, so its readers were cheerfully invited, if so inclined, to write those works themselves. In the same spirit, reading a film-text means that most of the work of imagining the film can be left to you, which is part of the fun of writing them.

B.S.
May Day
2015

1. INT. INSIDE PLANE.

Mark Ferry is looking out of an aeroplane porthole at thick clouds.
A circular rainbow is visible on the clouds.

Mark is English, about 24, and a not very seasoned traveller.

> ANNOUNCEMENT
> *(Italian accent)*
> We will shortly begin our descent to Rome
> Fiumicino Airport. The weather in Rome
> is unfortunately very heavy rain.
> The temperature is twenty-seven degrees.
> Please make sure your seat belt is fastened
> and your seat is in the upright position for landing.

2. INT. FIUMICINO AIRPORT.

Mark is standing uncertainly facing an intersection of several long
but largely deserted concrete walkways. He has a wheelie case,
a shoulder bag, and a medium-sized but heavy artist's portfolio.
He is perspiring from the heat. He finally chooses a direction.

3. INT. FIUMICINO AIRPORT.

Mark is standing facing a different intersection of several walkways,
again uncertain. He is clearly lost. He stops an Italian couple and
asks in stumbling and incorrect Italian:

> MARK
> Por favore, miscusi, ma dové il treni Leonardo
> Express—por Termini Stazione?

> MAN *(Italian accent, good English)*
> The Leonardo Express? I do not know.
> We are going to the car park. Try that way.
> Perhaps follow the T3 signs?

Mark sets off to follow T3 signs.

4. INT. FIUMICINO AIRPORT.

*Mark is standing facing yet another intersection of several walkways,
exasperated. Finally chooses a direction. And suddenly
finds the train platforms, including the Leonardo Express.*

5. INT. TERMINI STATION.

Rapid sequence of cuts:
*Mark follows the directions from the Leonardo Express platform 28 to
Metro Line A, which involves a longish walk through bustling crowds,
and includes several series of steps, up and down which he struggles with
his luggage, some unexpected turns of direction, and then baffling signs
taking him through the crowded Line B platform to the Line A
platform. He finally arrives, exasperated, at the right platform.*

6. EXT. OUTSIDE FLAMINIO METRO STATION.
VERY HEAVY RAIN.

*Mark stops a passing Italian woman and with a more practised
confidence (he has by now done this several times) asks:*

> MARK
> Per favore, Signora, dové la Via di Ripetta?

> ITALIAN WOMAN *(shrugs)*
> Non lo so. Una turista. Da Napoli. 'sera.

Mark shrugs and walks on in the pouring rain.

7. EXT. VIA DI RIPETTA. RAIN.

*Marks pauses for breath outside a shop window. He notices a sign in
the window: 'Puylaert Home Basics: Definitely your Home style' —
and behind the sign a collection of marble phalloi.
He laughs and walks on down the street in the pouring rain.*

8. EXT. VIA DI RIPETTA. RAIN.

The rain lashes down and Mark takes shelter in a shop, 'Il Mare',
devoted to everything to do with boats, ships, the sea.
Mark goes to the counter and asks the assistant,
who is eating a large slice of pizza:

> MARK
> Buonasera. Miscusi. Cerco il Lungotevere
> Tor di Nona. E 'dritto oa destra, per favore?

Assistant tries to answer but suddenly chokes on the pizza, nearly
vomits, rushes out of the door, and is promptly sick on the pavement.

> MARK *(to himself, as he leaves)*
> Non ci credo—mal di mare!?

10. EXT. OUTSIDE THE DOOR OF THE TEATRO TORDINONA. STILL RAINING.

Via degli Acquasparta, 16. Mark has finally arrived and is looking
exhausted. It is now early evening. Steady rain continues.

Either side of the small doorway of the Theatre are display windows on
which posters announce a production of Bertolt Brecht's Vita di
Galileo / Life of Galileo—but with banners announcing
LE PRESTAZIONI ANNULLATE [performance cancelled]
pasted across them.

A smaller poster also announces:

> ICONI DI SCIENZIA :
> ICONS OF SCIENCE
> Pale d'alterare : Altered Pieces
> Mostra d'arte di Mark Ferry
> Exhibition of art works by Mark Ferry

The whole theatre looks firmly closed and deserted.
Mark tries the doorhandle. Looks for a bell.

Finally he shouts through the letterbox.

>   MARK
> Qualcuno? Per favore?

Pause. An intercom on the door frame answers.

>   VOICE
> Chi c'è?

>   MARK
> Er, mi chiamo Mark Ferry.

>   VOICE
> *(pause)* The English artist?

>   MARK
> Sì.

>   VOICE
> Oh. *(pause)* Un momento. I will come.

A few seconds pass, then the door opens and ANGELINA appears.
She is Italian, early twenties and stunningly beautiful.
She speaks excellent English.

>   ANGELINA
> Mr Ferry? You have come. You did not get our text
> messages, our emails, our phone messages?

>   MARK
> *(he is very distracted by her beauty and flustered as well as*
> *exhausted)* Er, no. I've been very busy—before I left
> —finishing some new work—for the next show—
> *(he gestures at the portfolio, now soaked).* And then I
> miscalculated how to get here from the train station.
> I'm very sorry. I'm Mark, hello. Is there a problem?

ANGELINA

I see. *(pause)* You had better come in.
I am Angelina. Er, welcome.

11. INT. FOYER OF THE THEATRE.

Around the walls of the foyer are marks on the wall
where clearly about twenty smallish works have been recently hung.
But only the captions are now left.
Mark stands looking at the bare walls.

MARK

I see you've taken the show down already?

ANGELINA

Ah, si. Er, no, not quite. You have come
anyway—?

MARK

Well, I said I would come to oversee the move to
Naples for the next show. I couldn't get here for
the opening of this show, but I do prefer to be there
when they're hung. It matters how they're placed —

ANGELINA

You really did not get our emails? And we tried to
ring you, even today, but your mobile was off —

MARK

(he is gabbling, partly relieved to be able to speak English)
I was working pretty frantically up to the last
moment on a few new pieces, in case you'd sold
any, and I hate to be disturbed while I'm working,
so I haven't checked my emails for days. And I
loathe mobile phones. So, yes, sorry, I've been out
of touch. *(sudden thought)* Good Lord, you weren't
trying to tell me they'd *all* been sold, were you?
Is that why they're down, why you were trying to
contact me?

ANGELINA
Er, no, that's not it, I'm afraid. *(deep breath).*
We have not taken down your works, Mr Ferry.
Someone else did. I am sorry, Mr Ferry, to tell you
that your works have all been stolen.

MARK *(longish pause.)*
Well, I'm delighted!
I shall take that as a compliment!

ANGELINA *(baffled)*
Non capisco.

MARK *(enthusiastically)*
I've never had any of my stuff stolen before—
someone must really like it! Enough to steal it
anyway. *And* I get the insurance!
It's as if I'd sold the lot! So, it's fine by me—
don't look so worried, er, Angelina.
Pity about the next show, though. But, as they say,
Bless the Thief —he lightens you of your burden.
Now I don't have to sell any more of them. Great!
And do call me Mark, please.

ANGELINA
(she is still surprised at his reaction)
You do not understand, er, Mark—they were not
stolen because somebody *liked* them. But because
somebody *disliked* them, as they hated Brecht's play
about Galileo. It has been, er, difficult.

MARK
(still not understanding) Ah. I noticed the performance
had been cancelled. Bad run, was it?

ANGELINA
"Bad run"? I do not understand.

MARK
Nobody came, no tickets sold, poor reviews,
that kind of thing?

ANGELA
No, that was *not* the problem. I must explain.
(pause) But I think you might need a drink. Or two.
And you are very wet. There is a nice place just
around the corner. Bramante's Cloister.
We can go there.

12. INT. BALCONY OVERLOOKING COURTYARD.
RAINING STILL.

Angelina and Mark are seated with drinks on the balcony
overlooking the beautiful courtyard of the Chiostro del Bramante,
Arco della Pace, 5. Dusk.
Angelina has a laptop on. She has been explaining.

ANGELA
So, you did not see any of this on TV,
or in the newspapers?

MARK
Remember I don't read Italian and I've only just
arrived. And it certainly didn't make the English
news, I'm afraid

ANGELA
It was quite a big scandal here. It is on YouTube—
I will show you—this was 'the last stalk',
I think you say.

On her laptop she shows him recorded footage on Youtube—
[the images fill the cinema screen:

A fairly large and noisily excited crowd is outside the theatre
shouting slogans and waving banners proclaiming:

'*Abbasso Galile*', '*Abbasso Brecht*', '*Abbasso il comunismo*', '*Viva il Papa*', '*Abbasso blasfemia*' '*Viva la Sancta Ecclesia*'. [*Down with Galileo*', '*Down with Brecht*', '*Down with communism*', '*Support the pope*', '*Down with Blasphemy*'. *Long live Holy Church*']

ANGELINA

That went on during every performance for the whole first week. We finally had to cancel the play. We have been closed for three days now.
And then —the night before yesterday, someone came in and took all your paintings as well.

MARK

But—you *must* be joking!—these demos are a publicity stunt, yes?—for the rest of the tour— it must be!—nobody in their right minds can oppose Galileo in this day and age!

ANGELINA

No, Mark—it is *not* a publicity stunt—they were serious. Look, I will show you—the television interviewed some of them. Look.

(On the laptop: she shows the beginning of street interview with protestors, in Italian.)

MARK

I don't understand—

ANGELINA

Ah, yes—but one of the leaders is an American— you will understand him. Let me find him.

[on the laptop, but fills the cinema screen: a YouTube clip of a TV interview with Eamonn Boyle, large middle-aged American, a right-wing Catholic fundamentalist. Subtitles in Italian but we hear and see him shouting at the interviewer in English:

BOYLE

It's high time we stood up for Holy Mother Church.
She was *right* to *condemn* Galileo.
The Bible clearly says that the sun 'stood still'
at the Battle of Jericho —in black and white in
Joshua 10:13—that's what it *says* —
so the sun *must* normally *move*—around the earth,
as God wanted it to—we can even *see* it *move* with
our *own eyes*—and the good Lord would *not deceive*
His people about a thing like that, now would He.
Galileo should have read his *Bible*.

INTERVIEWER

So you really think the sun goes round the earth?
And do you also think that the earth was created
only six thousand years ago?

BOYLE

Indeed sir. That Charles Dawkins was just plain
wrong. He hasn't never read the Good Book
of the Lord, the Word of God. All modern science
is against the One True Word of God—
Newton, Galileo, that guy in the wheelchair—
what does he know!—and the Good Lord
has clearly inflicted him with sufferings for his
blasphemies.

INTERVIEWER

And so you think this play on the life of Galileo
is also a blasphemy?

BOYLE

Yessirree, it's by that Communist Atheist Bernard
Breckt—he's attacking my Holy Church,
and he's a godless unbeliever who will rot in Hell
when he dies—]

Angelina stops the video clip.

ANGELINA
And so on.

MARK
I'm baffled. I thought only fundamentalist
evangelicals went in for that kind of thing. But this
guy says he's supporting the Roman church—

ANGELINA
They think the new Pope will be one of them—
Remember that a fifth of Italians, and of Americans,
still think the sun goes round the earth—that's one
reason we decided to put on Brecht's play!

MARK
But now the run is cancelled—the play's
not going to Naples after all?

ANGELINA
It certainly is! It will open next week—
the theatre company has already gone ahead—
though these lunatic fundamentalists have
threatened to follow the production all round Italy.
That's why we first e-mailed you days ago—
to see if you didn't want the exhibition of your
paintings to travel to Naples with the play
after all—

MARK
I definitely do! Count me in ! but . . ah—

ANGELINA
Yes, then they were all stolen anyway.
So now, you would have to get them back first—
I think you may have had a wasted journey.

MARK

Well, I rather hope not!—*(he is clearly still dazzled by her)*—This is my first ever visit to Rome and I wasn't going to miss it. But what happens now? I thought I'd be packing up my show ready for the move to Naples late tomorrow. Are you going to Naples?

ANGELINA

No, I work for the Teatro di nona, not for the play company. I am the adminstrator who looks after touring companies. And I now have very little to do until the next company arrives in a week. So I am free to help you with the police inquiries and so on—the police tell us they are investigating —but they say the Christians absolutely deny it was them—they wouldn't steal, they claim—it's against the Bible, even if your paintings *are*, they say, idols and false images. But, I nearly forgot, there is one good news for you. You did actually sell one work.

MARK

Great! Which one?

ANGELINA

It was the one called Hypatia. But of course that was then stolen with the rest.

MARK

(ruefully, jokingly) So I won't even get the money for that one, either. It might have paid for my trip!

ANGELINA

But you will, perhaps. The man who bought it is a very old friend of the theatre, and he said he would much like to meet you. He says he even has a 'proposition' for you. And he offered to put you up, if you came. Did you book anywhere else to stay?

MARK

I was beginning to worry about that, actually.
It's getting late and I haven't booked in anywhere,
because the theatre said they'd be able to put me up.

ANGELINA

Yes, we did. I will ring Signor Noé to see if it's OK.
Tomorrow you will have to meet the police—
and the insurance people—and Signor Bertolli,
the gallery owner who sponsored your exhibition. I
think he's not pleased that the works were all stolen.

MARK

I have to meet all these people tomorrow?
Well, I've booked myself a timed ticket to the
Vatican museums for tomorrow afternoon,
so I hope I don't have to miss that. Otherwise,
I'm free, in your hands, I hope. But where's this
place I'm staying? You said his name was Noè?
And he had a 'proposition' for me?

ANGELINA

Yes, Signor Noè. But let him explain.
He's got a huge house just by the river—
'Il segno dell'arcobaleno'.

MARK

Il segno dell'— what?

ANGELINA

The sign of the rainbow—I think it was a hotel
once, many years ago. He's got acres of rooms.
But few people ever get inside it these days.
You're very privileged!

MARK
Fine, lead on. I can get out of these wet clothes
at least. And see if my new pieces have survived
the rain. It's not much to make a new show out of,
but it's a start!

13. EXT. OUTSIDE THE HUGE HOUSE OF NOÈ.
LIGHT RAIN. NEARLY DARK. [Via della Rondinella, 2]

*Mark is standing with his luggage. Angelina knocks at the large door.
It is quickly opened by a very old but sprightly man in a long flowing
gown. He has a full white beard, a bald head and rather ancient
glasses. He speaks perfect English as well as Italian.*

ANGELINA
Buonasera, Signor Noè. Let me introduce
Mr Mark Ferry. You can still put him up for the
night, yes? It will be no trouble?

*Noè kisses her elegantly and warmly on both cheeks,
then equally warmly shakes Mark's hand.*

NOÈ
Buonasera, signorina Angelina, la mia più bella
cara— And the very wet Mr Ferry. Welcome,
indeed. No trouble at all, no trouble at all.
Have you eaten? Would you like a warm bath?
Something to drink perhaps?

MARK
This is very generous of you, Mr Noè. I'm fine—
though I am, I'm afraid, a little wet.

ANGELINA
Signor Noè, I really must go now. Mark, I shall
leave you safely with Signor Noè—but please come
to the theatre at around ten tomorrow and I'll take
you to the police, the insurance, Bertolli, and so on.
OK? Ciao—

Noè kisses Angelina affectionately on both cheeks as they say goodbye.
Mark hesitates a moment, then somewhat clumsily attempts to kiss her
also on both cheeks, not very successfully.

MARK
Ciao, Angelina. I'll see you tomorrow, I hope.

ANGELINA
Ciao, ciao! Arrivederci. Addio Signor Noè.

NOÈ
Now, do come in out of the rain, Mr Ferry.
Though, personally, I love the rain. I've always
found it somehow most comforting.

14. INT. LARGE DINING ROOM. DIMLY LIT.

Mark is seated at a huge dining room table, with the remains of a
generous cold meal of various fresh vegetables, good bread, cheese and
fruit before him. Mark is now dressed in a borrowed and vaguely
oriental dressing gown, is bathed and dry and is fairly sleepy. He has
a large wine goblet in his hand, as does Noè, also seated at the table.

NOÈ
(opening another dusty bottle)
Now this wine is one of my favourites.
Horace sang its praises once. Though the vintages
have never been quite as good again as in his days,
I'm afraid. Do try a glass or two.

MARK
Signor Noè, I am overwhelmed by your hospitality.
I feel absolutely satisfied already. *(hesitates)*
But, by all means, yes, I can't resist.

NOÈ
It has to be drunk. Why keep a wine cellar
till the end of days. It would be a shameful waste.

He pours Mark more wine, into another goblet.

NOÈ

Now, Mark, if I may, a question. That work of
yours I bought, but sadly lost to some wickedly
discerning thief, it was of Hypatia, yes. But who
was your model, if I may be so inquisitive?

MARK

Hypatia, yes. The Alexandrian philosopher.
I wanted some women thinkers among my icons of
science. But there was no live model for the work,
I'm afraid, just my own imagination and memory.

NOÈ

Ah, so you had never seen Hypatia, then?

MARK

Hardly, Mr Noè, she died in the fourth century A.D.

NOÈ

Of course. Of course. And you are not that old,
surely. Yes. *(pause)* A dreadful end. Torn to pieces,
flayed alive, by a Christian mob, for being a pagan
woman and an original thinker. *(pause)*
I meant, of course, did you have a living woman
in mind when you painted her?

MARK
(he is slurring a little by now)
My science icons are not really paintings, you know,
Mr Noè, more like collages, combining images from
books, prints, scientific textbooks, and the like.
My Hypatia was partly composed from a famous
Fayyum portrait—a very beautiful second century
image that was once even thought to be of Hypatia,
but actually isn't, of course—*(he is rambling a little)*—
but I do have that Fayyum portrait on my camera
still, if you want to see that.

Mark gets up from the table, with some difficulty, and goes to his
shoulder bag in the corner, takes his camera from a side pocket, and
slowly finds the image as he comes back to Noe. He shows it to Noe.

Noe looks for a long time at the image (the Fayyum face)
on the camera, which silently fills the cinema screen.

> NOÈ
>
> No, I do agree. I don't think that's her, after all.
> Sadly. But that's not quite how she looked in your
> own work, is it? The one I bought, and lost.
> She looked a little different, yes.

> MARK
>
> *(slurring)* You're quite right. You see, that's because I
> sort of blended that image with a retouched version
> of the Mona Lisa itself, which I reversed and
> modified a little. I have that one somewhere too.
> Let me find it.

Mark takes another drink of the wine as he flicks through his camera's
images, and then shows Noè another image, which again fills the screen
for a moment, as Noè looks long and hard at it.

> NOÈ
>
> Ah, yes. Yes. That was it. Of course.
> She looked just a little older by then.
> But beautiful, beautiful, still. As always. *(pause)*
> I do so miss her.

> MARK
>
> *(a bit alarmed at this, tries to change the topic)*
> Er, Miss Angelina mentioned something
> about a proposition, Mr Noè. Is that right?

NOÈ

Yes indeed, my dear boy. How shall I put it?
Let me see. It was not *your* fault that I do not now
have your painting of Hypatia, or *le collage*, *kollazh*
(he pronounces the word as French, then as Russian) —
which I bought so readily, so I am quite happy
to pay you for it, nevertheless. Say, two thousand
euros—

MARK

But, I, I only priced it at five hundred—

NOÈ

(continues, but he too is clearly now somewhat drunk)
No matter—but in addition to that,
would you perhaps consider painting for me—
you do actually *paint*, do you not, with oils, properly,
if I may so indelicately put it?—another, but larger
version of your Hypatia, or should I say *my* Hypatia,
one more perhaps shaped, guided, by *my* memory,
or *my*, er, imagination. I would be more than happy
for you to work here, in my house, as in the old
days, for as long as you need or wish, and I would
also pay you well—

MARK

I am most honoured, Mr Noè—and I would be
delighted—but perhaps in the cold light of day,
you might wish to—

NOÈ

I have too few cold lights of days left, I think,
in which to—reconsider, as you were perhaps about
to suggest. Would you accept the commission?

MARK

With great pleasure, yes indeed.

NOÈ
Then let me show you to your studio,
and then back to your room.

*Noè is clearly very drunk by now, as is Mark, but they weave their
way out of the dining room.*

15. INT. LARGE ATTIC ROOM. LARGE ROOF
WINDOWS. DARK NIGHT.

*In the middle of the room is a very old-fashioned wooden easel,
and a long table with several dozen mixing and grinding bowls,
dozens of jars of coloured pigments, several bottles of liquid, some old
palettes, sea shells for paint mixing, and several brushes. Leaning
against the wall are canvasses of various sizes, their faces to the wall.
There are also a few old wooden boards, a small old-fashioned stove and
some cooking pots. Mark looks amazed at all this ancient equipment.*

NOÈ
I think you will have everything you need here.
I don't know which method you prefer, but there is
walnut, linseed, and poppy-seed oils, some honey—
though Leonardo preferred to add simple beeswax,
if I recall aright—vinegar, some white lead—
Rubens always used walnut oil with lead oxide—
but I believe that is now out of fashion. And the
pigments are the finest I still have—of course you
cannot get proper yellows from India any more.
Or genuine lapis lazuli, I am afraid. Do feel free to
re-use any of the canvasses if it saves time.
I no longer have much need of them.

MARK
(bewildered and sobering up) I'm not quite, er, sure,
Mr Noè, that I can handle this equipment.

NOÈ
I'm sure you will feel more up to it in the morning,
my dear boy. I do assure you it's good material.
Mainly from Annibale, I think—or was it Sanzio
gave me some of it? Any rate, please do not worry
—and I strongly suggest the very first light. It can
be quite magnificent up here at four in the morning.
Meanwhile, your room. A few hours sleep will do
you the world of good, young Mark, if I may so
address you. And do help yourself to breakfast in
the dining room at whatever time you please.

MARK
Certainly. Yes, yes, I do need some sleep, I think.
Or to wake up.

16. INT. LARGE BEDROOM. MORNING LIGHT.

Mark wakes up, looks around, befuddled, with heavy hangover.
Looks at his watch. 8 a.m.

17. INT. CORRIDOR.

Mark, now fully dressed, is lost, looking for the dining room.
He opens a doorway.

The door opens onto a long room, with window shutters closed, barely
lit. In the gloom, dozens of stuffed animals in glass cases, not all of
them instantly recognisable. Dozens of animal heads on the walls.

Mark closes the door and wanders down the corridor.
Opens another door.

A large room, also barely lit from shuttered windows.
Leaning against the walls are several large wooden painted crucifixes.
On the walls are several large paintings. Mark gasps in surprise,
then takes his camera from his pocket and takes a quick photo.

Mark closes the door and wanders further down the corridor.
Opens another door.

A huge library, with bookcases to the ceiling. Books piled everywhere.
Very dusty.

Mark closes the door and shakes his head firmly,
trying to shake off the hangover. At the end of the long corridor,
he comes to an elegant staircase leading up and down. He heads down.

18. INT. THE LARGE DINING ROOM.

Mark enters and sees Noè spread-eagled on the floor, deeply asleep,
clutching an very old empty wine bottle, and snoring heavily.
Noè's gown has opened and he is naked underneath the gown.
Mark carefully covers him over and tiptoes into the adjoining kitchen.

19. INT. LARGE OLD-FASHIONED KITCHEN.

Mark finds old-fashioned coffee equipment, including a grinder.
He hesitates, then loudly grinds coffee beans.

20. INT. DINING ROOM.

Noè has woken with the sound of the grinder, bleary-eyed.
Mark enters with cups and a steaming coffee pot.

> MARK
> Good morning, Signor Noè. I've made some coffee.
> Would you like some?

> NOÈ
> Good morning, young Mark. Black coffee would
> be lovely. I trust you slept well. Have you begun the
> painting? The dawn was quite beautiful.

MARK

I'm afraid sir, that I slept rather too well.
I've only just woken up. And must apologise—
I have to meet the police in an hour, about the theft
of my work, so I'm afraid I will have to start the
painting rather later than I'd planned.

NOÈ

No matter. Ah, this coffee is good.
(sips it appreciatively) You know, there was nothing
quite like that very first taste of coffee.
(in Arabic:) qahhwat al-bun—wine of the bean.
It was quite a rival for a time. But real wine always
wins in the end. *(shakes his hung-over head)*
At a price, of course.
So, when do you wish to begin, Mark?
Once you have prepared the canvas,
I have some small suggestions for the painting itself.

MARK

Ah, yes. Er, I was wondering, Signor Noè,
if you happen to have a copy of, say,
Cennini's *Treatise on Painting*, or perhaps Vasari—
I rather need to refresh my memory a little,
about oil techniques—it's been quite a while.
And I noticed you have a wonderful library upstairs.

NOÈ

Of course, dear boy. I do understand. Oil painting
is not what it was. I will go and find something
suitable for you. I do have a few of those manuals,
I remember. Yes, indeed. So, you'll find bread and
fruit in the cold pantry, next to the wine cellar door.
Help yourself.

Noè leaves. Mark sips coffee thoughtfully.

21. INT. DINING ROOM.

Mark has a plate of half eaten bread, fruit, cheese in front of him.

Noè enters with an armful of books and manuscripts.
He puts them on the table in front of Mark.

> NOÈ
> These might be useful to you. Let me just get some
> breakfast while you consult them.

Noè goes to the kitchen while Mark opens the books and looks at the
manuscripts.

Close-ups of the books and title pages as Mark opens them:

They include: Trattato della Pittura messo in Luce la prima Volta con
Annotazioni dal Giuseppe Tambroni. Cennino Cennini,. Roma,
Paolo Salviucci, 1821. (A large octavo, bound in blue boards,
with broad margins, printed on fine heavy paper.)

Vom Alter der Oelmalerey aus dem Theophilus Presbyter, Gotthold
Ephraim Lessing. (A thin brown-paper-bound booklet, with
the publisher indicated as Buchhandlung des Fürstlichen
Waysenhauses, 1774.)

A Treatise on Painting written by Cennino Cennini in the year 1437;
and first published in Italian in 1821, with an introduction and notes,
by Signor Tambroni: containing practical directions for painting in
fresco, secco, oil and distemper, with the art of gilding and illuminating
manuscripts adopted by the old Italian Masters, translated by Mrs
Merrifield, with an introductory preface, copious notes, and illustrations
in outline from celebrated pictures. Published by Edward Lumley,
London, 1844. (A large quarto bound in cream cloth,
resembling vellum, with ornate gilt tooling on spine, back &
front covers. All edges gilt.)

Le vite de' più eccellenti pittori, scultori e architettori, Firenze, 1550
(Old vellum bound, bent covers).

One manuscript is in Latin, in crabbed handwriting,
with a cover page, on which is written in a florid later hand:
'Rogerus de Helmarshausen scripsit, De diversis artibus.'

Another manuscript is in beautifully ornate Italian handwriting,
illuminated in the margins. On the top right corner is written,
in very faded ink: 'Vasari'.

Noè comes back with a glass of red wine and an open bottle.

> MARK
> These are amazing.

> NOÈ
> Yes, I rather like the Vasari. It was a present.
> Though he was wrong about Van Eyck.
> I often said so. I had checked it with
> Cardinal Albergati, of course.

> MARK
> I would love to look at these later, Signor Noè.
> But I have to go now. And *(hesitates)*
> I wonder if you would mind terribly if I used, erm,
> somewhat more modern methods of—

> NOÈ
> Not at all, not at all. Every generation of artists
> has its own way of working, I know that.
> Fashions do change. Sometimes it's tempera,
> next it's oil, then mosaic comes back in,
> or people prefer fresco to panel painting, or *vice versa*.
> Always changing. Temperament, I suppose.
> So, we will talk more later, but off you go.
> Please join me for dinner if you can. My meals are
> lonely these days and I would welcome your company.
> I dine at eight. Cold food, I'm afraid. I haven't
> cooked since my dear wife—But don't keep the lovely
> Angelina waiting. She said ten o'clock, did she not?

22. EXT. ON BRIDGE TO PALAZZO DI JUSTITIA.

*Mark and Angelina are walking across the bridge
towards the Palazzaccio.*

MARK
I may be getting out of my depth with Signor Noè.
Do you know where I can buy some prepared
canvas, some oil paints, brushes—an artists'
materials shop? I think I spotted one in the
Via di Ripetta on the way here.

ANGELINA
Not my territory. I buy books not paints.
But that would make sense, near the Accademia.
We can try to find it later.

23. INT. OFFICE [INSIDE PALAZZO DI IUSTITIA.]

*Luigi Contardo, a junior police detective, is seated at a desk covered
with files. On chairs in front of the desk are Mark and Angelina.
Contardo speaks poor English. He is obviously bored.
The meeting has lasted a short time already.*

CONTARDO
So, Signor Ferry, we have done what is possibile.
The Christian *(consults a note)* Truth Mission say they
do not have your paintings. And your paintings are
not worth very much time, we think. It is only a
small thieving. So it is not really my department.

ANGELINA
But your department deals with art thefts.
That's why we came to you, not just the local police.

CONTARDO
Ah, yes, art thefts, but we mean, in Rome,
important art works, Roman antiquities,
masterpieces. You are not Michelangelo, Mr Ferry.

MARK

Maybe not. But my works are valuable to me.
And I just sold one for two thousand euros.

CONTARDO
(lifts his eyebrows and glances over the catalogue on his desk)
Two thousand, you say. But your prices are only
three or five hundred euros in the exhibition.
Are you perhaps, *come dice*, egging, er, exaggerating,
Signor Ferry—for the insurance—?

ANGELINA

That's an outrageous suggestion —

MARK

Well, Signor Noè may be eccentric but that's what
he said he'd pay me—and twenty works at
two thousand euros would be 40,000 euros—
that's not such a small thieving—

CONTARDO
(has become suddenly alert) Yes. Perhaps. *(pause)*
You say Signor Noè bought your work—
you know Signor Noè?

MARK

Yes, I'm staying with him, and he has commissioned
me to do a painting for him.

CONTARDO

One moment, Signor Ferry. *(pauses)*
Let me consult a colleague.
Perhaps your case will interest him after all.

Contardo leaves the office.

MARK
Why the sudden change?

ANGELINA
It's clearly Noè he's interested in, not your work,
I think. But why I don't know.

MARK
Who *is* Noè? How long have you known him?

ANGELINA
About three years. Ever since I started working
for the theatre. I called on him once, fund-raising
for a production. He seemed to like me, and he's
been friendly ever since. He came to your show
because I invited him. I feel sorry for him.
And a bit worried about him—he seems very
depressed recently.

MARK
I'm not sure if he drinks because he's depressed,
or he's depressed because he drinks—

Contardo returns and interrupts.

CONTARDO
If, Signor Ferry, we discover anything of your
works, can we contact you at Signor Noè's?
At Via della Rondinella, yes? My colleague,
Detective Inspector Zoretti, is busy now
but asks you please to see him tomorrow.
He will interest in your case. His office, here, please,
at nine tomorrow morning please.
That will suit you?

MARK
Fine. I'll be here.

24. EXT. CAFFE DI CAPITOLINO.
THE TERRACE RESTAURANT.

Mark, Angelina, and Bertolli are seated with coffees and mineral
water. There is a glorious view of Rome towards Vatican City.
It has stopped raining. A beautiful day.

Bertolli is a gallery owner and art dealer, confident, middle-aged, very
well-dressed Italian. Speaks excellent English.

> BERTOLLI
> If we get your work back, Mark, I must put your
> prices up. Old Noè used to be pretty well known in
> gallery circles. And he has a good eye.
> Perhaps I underestimated your sale value.
> I shall certainly push Donizone on the point
> anyway. Here he comes.

Donizone comes to join them. He is the insurance representative,
careful, non-committal, soberly dressed, carrying a fashionably
slim briefcase. He bows politely to Angelina, then sits
and gestures to the waiter for a coffee.

> BERTOLLI
> Ah, Donizone, I'll introduce you—Mark Ferry,
> the artist—Angelina De Luca, administrator for
> Teatro Tordinona. They've just come from il
> Dipartimento per i Furti d'Arte, but they report no
> progress on recovery yet. May we speak in English
> for Mark's benefit.

> DONIZONE
> Prego.

> MARK
> Si. Scusi, ma non parlo Italiano. Un poco, un miu
> poco, poco.

BERTOLLI
(ignores Mark's attempt at humour, and addresses Donizone with some hostility) You will have to pay up, you know.

DONIZONE
It is early, of course.

BERTOLLI
But, I remind you, there is already the loss of *potential* sales—the Mark Ferry exhibition was due to open in Naples this coming week and I will have to cancel that—and without the exhibition of course we can't sell—also there will be expenses involved in that cancellation, of course.

MARK *(timidly)*
Well, I do have three new ones—
not enough for a full show, of course, but—

DONIZONE
Signor Bertolli, you know that we cannot consider a claim for loss of potential sales without any actual sales as evidence for potential sales.
How many works were sold? One, I believe.

BERTOLLI
On the very first day—for a price well above the listed price. My client is paying two thousand euros.

DONIZONE
(raises a cynical eyebrow) Indeed? But that is irrelevant. You are insured for the prices in the catalogue. Three to five hundred per work.

BERTOLLI *(getting aggressive)*
But those low prices were simply to launch a new artist. I can now sell Mark's work at a much higher rate, and that should obviously be the value we are talking about for insurance. The value of a work of

art is what it will sell for in the open market, not some estimated price in a catalogue.

DONIZONE
If you recover the works, then we *may* renegotiate the policy, and the premium, for the future.
But of course we will not consider any change in the present policy.

BERTOLLI
But you will pay up?

DONIZONE
Only after one year.

MARK
(semi-joking) What? I don't even get the insurance money for a year?

DONIZONE
Signor Ferry, *you* would not receive the insurance money in any case. Our contract is with Signor Bertolli's gallery. I will explain however. Any allegedly stolen or missing work has to be missing for a year and a day. We then *consider* the claim. That is the standard contract.

BERTOLLI
But that is not in the contract for this exhibition. I specifically excluded that clause, I remind you, Donizone.

DONIZONE
(opens his briefcase and rapidly consults a file) I see. In that case, we must have positive evidence that the works are missing.

ANGELINA
(intervenes into what is becoming a hostile exchange)
I don't understand, Signor Donizone.
What positive evidence could we provide?
You cannot prove a negative.

DONIZONE
Can you prove that the works were stolen?
Is there CCTV footage of the theft? Witnesses?
You may have simply hidden them.
And then claimed the insurance.

ANGELINA
Signor Donizone, you are talking about one of the
oldest theatres in Rome. Are you really accusing us
of attempting a fraud.

DONIZONE
It is my job to prevent fraud, or false claims.
I have checked with the police. They have no
evidence of a theft.
BERTOLLI *(angry)*
If they did they would have evidence of who did it.
This is absurd.

DONIZONE *(ice-cold)*
That is my position. You may contact me if the
situation changes.

He gets to his feet, bows politely to Angelina, and starts to leave.
Bertolli stands and angrily confronts him.

BERTOLLI
Between you and the police, I'm going to have to
find the works myself!

DONIZONE
I suggest you do that.

BERTOLLI
You haven't paid for your coffee, Donizone.

MARK *(intervenes)*
Come dice: 'this round is on me?' 'Il mio turno?'

ANGELINA *(smiles)*
Offro io—

DONIZONE
Grazie, Signor Ferry. Signorina. Arriverderci.

Donizone leaves. Bertolli sits angrily in silence.

MARK
Look, er, I'm going to have to go shortly.
In fifty minutes I have a timed entry ticket for the
Vatican Museums and I am *not* going to waste that.
I had to book it online and I gather that the queues
are pretty horrendous otherwise. So—shall I get the
bill? *(He waves to a waiter)* Il conto, pervarotti.

ANGELINA
(giggles at this malapropism) Mark, yes, you go.
I will pay the bill. And if you want to buy those
artists' materials, we could meet later. Can you be at
the main entrance to the Castel Sant'Angelo at five?
I will find out where the best shops are by then.

MARK
Fine. Goodbye, Signor Bertolli. I will see you again,
no doubt.

BERTOLLI
I will find your damn paintings myself if necessary.

MARK
Ciao, Angelina.

He tries not very successfully to kiss her on both cheeks and then leaves.

25. EXT. VIA LEONE IV.

Mark passes the very very long queue for the entrance to the Vatican Museums.

26. INT. THE SISTINE CHAPEL.

Mark is squashed onto a side bench in a corner of the chapel, gazing upward at the ceiling. A long take.

27. INT. SAINT PETER'S BASILICA.
NEAR THE PIETA.

Mark is standing near the packed crowd of tourists all trying to take photos of Michelangelo's Pieta.

Mark takes a photo of the tourists taking photos. Then shrugs and fights his way out of the basilica.

28. EXT. OUTSIDE ENTRANCE TO
CASTEL SANT' ANGELO.

Mark is waiting. Angelina approaches him and kisses him warmly on both cheeks.

                ANGELINA
So, how were the Vatican Museums?

                MARK
(still recovering from the kiss, and unsure)
Well, the Sistine Chapel is extraordinary. Stunning. Immense. Do I have anything to add to what's been said so often? I was in awe.

                ANGELINA
And the rest?

MARK

I think the correct word is 'chiusa'.
The Salle de Raphael : 'chiusa'.
The Appartemente Borgia : 'chiusa'.
The Museo Gregoriano : 'chiusa'.
The Etruscan museum : 'chiusa'.
I saw the Pinacoteca, though—
and the boats, which I didn't know about.

ANGELINA

Ah, you have learned a very important Italian word.
Chiusa. Closed. Italy is often closed. But the boats?
What boats?

MARK

Well, I walked up that long curving stairway
to the first floor, rather than take the escalator,
which was horribly packed. And on the side
of the stairway is this crazy collection of boats,
of every size, age, shape—all models, of course,
but I've never seen such a collection.

ANGELINA

I don't remember the boats. But there is so much to
see—when it is not chiusa! Now, I have two shops
for you. The first is fairly near, the Belle Arti
Lizzani, in Viale Angelico, and the other is near the
theatre, Green Point, in Via della Scrofa. Choose.

MARK

Let's go for the nearest.

ANGELINA

But, first, we just have time for one of my favourite
spots in Rome. And for another vey important
Italian word. 'Un prosecco.'

29. INT. SMALL ALCOVE ON THE HIGH TERRACE OF CASTEL SANT' ANGELO.

Mark and Angelina are seated, with drinks and appetizers. It is a balmy evening. As they drink, relaxed, taking their time:

ANGELINA
I liked your work, Mark—before it was stolen—but I wasn't sure I understood it.

MARK
To be honest, there isn't that much to 'understand' about the work itself. It's just simple collage. But it is *about* things we *don't* fully understand, or about the problem of understanding, if you like —I wanted to explore some relations between science and religion by treating famous figures of science as quasi-religious icons, as if they were the saints of an old, or perhaps of a new, religion—but also reminding people that, well, religion has, or had, its own claims to truth, that it was once a way of *trying* to understand the world, in its own terms. That's partly what I think Brecht's play on Galileo is about, which is why I was so pleased to have my work accompany that production.

ANGELINA
But Brecht doesn't see Galileo as some kind of saint? He's more like a failure, he gives in to the inquisition. All they had to do was show him the instruments of torture.

MARK
But that's the point. 'Pity the land that has need of heroes.' Scientists aren't heroes, but they shouldn't *need* to be either. Brecht saw Galileo's time as a brief historical moment when the new science might have

linked hands with the people, with popular needs and democratic demands, a growing revolt against the old powers and authorities. In the play, Galileo recognises that new thinking comes from practical people, from workers on the docks, in the shipyards, in the metal factories, in the arsenal. But then he betrays that moment—he recants and retreats into private research, under the control of the church, those same authorities—it's the moment when science became separated off from the people, so that eventually, as Brecht saw it, we allow the scientists to invent even worse instruments of murder and terror than the inquisition ever had— Brecht re-wrote the play in the shadow of the atomic bomb. We trusted the scientists to get on with their work, without understanding or controlling what they were doing, and they created a terrible monster.

ANGELINA
So why did you present them as saints, as religious icons?

MARK
Because now we've lost faith in them.
They've lost our trust and when they do actually warn us of real coming catastrophes, of global warming and the extinction of humanity itself, we just don't believe them, any more than we now believe the old religions. Science has become a faith we've lost faith in. We only admire their relics without even understanding them.

ANGELINA
You know, you nearly sold your Galileo icon to Noè as well as the Hypatia. But he said something about him looking too old.

MARK

Well, I don't know what he meant by that. My
Galileo was based on a contemporary print of him.
Any rate, I used the iconographic conventions of
how to depict saints and martyrs and adapted them
to Newton, Darwin, Einstein, Faraday, and the rest,
giving each his emblems, how we identify them,
so Newton has his apple and Darwin his worms,
as St Peter has his upside down cross. And they're
carrying scrolls with their most famous equations or
statements on them, just like the saints with their
quotations from the bible—but in fact we no longer
know what those equations mean—they're just
icons of rationality, a new kind of magic. We've all
heard of ' $E=mc^2$ ' but how many people could
begin to explain what it really means—or even what
Paul Dirac's equations actually were? Scientific
achievements are just the enshrined altarpieces of
today—and to most people they're just as strange or
remote or baffling as the old saints are to us now.

ANGELINA

But your pun doesn't really work in Italian—
you called them 'Altered Pieces', like altar-pieces —
but it took me some time to get the joke.

MARK

It's not a joke, though. We do now have this sort of
credulity about 'Science', but many of us don't
have a clue what scientists actually do.
ust as most of us don't really know what artists do
or did, but sort of accept that 'art' must somehow
be important. This afternoon I watched hundreds
of people taking photos of Michelangelo's Pieta,
but I bet very few could have told me *why* it is or
was important—and they certainly couldn't be
looking at it properly while jammed in with
hundreds of others, all dragooned into tour groups
and following a waving flag or umbrella.

I got out of Saint Peter's as fast as I could.
I simply loathed that overweening basilica,
with its baroque triumphalism, its exaggerted
emotional statues, its childish 'I'm bigger than
you are' attitude, and its basically spatch-cocked
architectural compromises. But the crowds flock
there because they've been told it's 'a masterpiece'.
And with packed crowds like that,
even the Sistine Chapel was almost intolerable.

ANGELINA
Ah, the snobbery of the true artist.
You are a tourist, *I* am a discerning traveller!
You are ticking off a 'must-see' object listed in your
guide book, but *I* am appreciating a work of art.
But what is "spatch-cocked" anyway? *(teasing)*
Is it erotic?

MARK
Don't scoff, Angelina. I take your point,
but it's a real problem. Look, I talked to a woman
from Texas in the cafe in the Vatican.
At *huge* expense she'd flown the Atlantic to bring
her teenage daughter with her to Rome
and they'd booked a *de luxe* four-hour tour of the
Vatican Museums. After two hours she realised
that her daughter was no longer listening to the
guide's commentary on the earphones they all had
to put on, but was listening to her own pop music
on her i-pod instead. The mother was furious.
But I can see the daughter's point.
When I asked her, she said she simply hadn't a clue
what the guide was talking about—all those endless
details about which saint was which, and how to
recognise them from what they were carrying or
how they were dressed, which Pope had
commissioned which artist to decorate which bit of

which room, which artist had influenced which
other artist, which one had used some new
technique, which painting had been restored, which
statue had been erected in which pope's reign.
The girl was simply bored out of her mind—
but this was 'Culture', this was 'Art', and her mother
had paid a helluva lot for it and she'd better damn
well listen. It was hopeless. So I asked the mother
if she could name any three consecutive
Renaissance Popes. She couldn't. I then asked her
if that made any difference to her life.
She had to say it really didn't. I agreed.

            ANGELINA
So . . . ?

            MARK
So then I invited them back into the Pinacoteca
and showed them a little portrait of Voltaire,
tucked away in a corner, and told them a bit about
Voltaire, whom they'd never heard of. I sketched his
influence on the Enlightenment and therefore on
the Founding Fathers of America. And so on.
But mainly I asked them just to stand quietly and
really *look* at that portrait, that face, for a whole five
minutes—and perhaps think of how Voltaire was
maybe smiling that wicked grin because he was
actually in the Vatican Museum, of all places!
Enough.

            ANGELINA
Alright, enough. We'd better get to your shop
before it closes. But tomorrow, as an antidote
to the horrible Saint Peter's, I will take you to my
own favourite church in Rome, to San Clemente.
OK?

            MARK
San Clemente? Delighted.

30. EXT. OUTSIDE BELLE ARTI LIZZANI
[Viale Angelico, 259]

MARK

Will you come in and translate for me?
I want to ask about various oils and prepared
canvases. And I need to know if they stock some
quick-drying oil paints, maybe some Griffin Alkyd,
or even slow drying acrylics, Golden Open
or Chroma Atelier Interactive—

ANGELINA

I haven't a clue what you're talking about, Mark.
In any case, you should learn to cope in Italian.
You might want to work, or even live here—
sometime.

MARK *(looking at her)*
Well, it would certainly have its attractions.
Alright, I'll give it a go.

Angelina waits, patiently, and amused.

*Mark re-appears, successfully loaded with various materials,
canvasses, brushes, oil paints, a palette.*

MARK

Right, got the lot. Now I must get to work.
I have to finally make a start. And I promised Noè I
would join him for dinner tonight.
But may I take you to dinner tomorrow, Angelina,
after we've been to San Clemente?

ANGELINA

Yes. You may. But remember you have to
meet the policeman tomorrow at nine.

MARK

God, yes, I'd forgotten. What was his name?

ANGELINA

Detective Inspector Zoretti. I can't be there.
I have to liaise with people from the next
production company first thing tomorrow.
But I can meet you later, at the theatre around
eleven, yes? And we can go to San Clemente.

MARK

I look forward to it. A lot.

Angelina gives him a brief kiss on both cheeks.

ANGELINA

Ciao, Mark.

31. INT. ATTIC STUDIO IN NOAH'S HOUSE.

*Noè is showing several canvas portraits of women to Mark, one after
the other. Each is familiar to him as a well-known art work.
Mark is growing more and more astonished.
Noè is fairly drunk and is talking sentimentally.*

NOÈ

Of course, any painter can paint a pretty face,
but some can do the eyebrows well, another gets
the lips right, maybe another paints perfect ears,
or the line of the neck. But they never *really* got her
right, any of them. But then your Hypatia was *almost*
there—and I realised why, when you explained
about combining Hypatia with Lisa. That was pretty
close, Mark, I can tell you. But can you do even
better? Can you take the best of *all* these—these are
sort of failures, but they *are* my favourites of her—
and really show me what she looked like?
Can you do that, Mark?

MARK

I'm a bit baffled, Signor Noè. Am I trying to paint
Hypatia, or what? And where did these
extraordinary copies come from?

NOÈ

No, no, not Hypatia. No. Hypatia just reminded
me. You see, they were good friends once,
in Alexandria, and they were sometimes even
mistaken for each other—so of course we had
to leave quickly after that dreadful day. Horrible.

MARK

I'm really no wiser, Signor Noè. *(cautiously)*
And about these copies—?

NOÈ

Do just call me Noè. *(pause)* Are they copies?
I can't remember. Some of them are, yes.
They were all, well, presents. I used to ask
for copies. But is an original copy a copy?
I don't know. I'm a bit ashamed, I admit, but
they rarely paid her. It was the least I could ask.

MARK *(gently)*

Who is 'she', Noè?

NOÈ

My wife, of course, Mark. She had several names
—Emzara, Haykêl, Barthenos, Nemzar, Set—
but I always called her Naamah, the beautiful one.

MARK

Noè, are you telling me that these paintings
are all portraits of your wife?

NOÈ

Yes, Mark, yes! They would come and drink in
my Rainbow Sign, the bar, the inn, the herberg,
posada, locanda, Kneipe—whichever country
we were in —and they would ogle her, and she
would be flattered, as always. And then she would
agree to pose as their model, so she said.

I had to believe that was all it was. But I always
asked for a copy. Even when they painted her nude.
But I didn't keep those. I couldn't bear to.

MARK *(very gently)*
And the Mona Lisa, Noè? That too?

NOÈ
Of course. 'La mia Lisa', he called her. But I don't
have my copy of that one. Naamah took it herself.
She loved that painting. Last time I saw it was in
Paris. Or in London. I can't remember.

MARK
(almost a joke) So tell me, Noè, why was your wife
smiling that strange smile?

NOÈ
It amused her that Leonardo was so besotted with
a woman several thousand years old. She was trying
not to giggle. Can you paint her, Mark?
Can you paint her? *(pause)* I need a drink.

MARK
I can try.

*Noè starts to leave unsteadily. He stops, takes something
from the pocket of his gown and comes back.*

NOÈ
Would you please paint her wearing this?
It was her favourite piece of jewellery.
I bought it for her in Susa, a long time ago. *(pause)*
Come down to dinner in an hour or so.

Noè hands Mark a necklace. It is made of pearls and very beautiful.

Noè leaves. Mark gazes at the necklace.

32. INT. ATTIC STUDIO.

*Mark has lined up the various canvas portraits of women against the
wall and table. He carefully takes a close-up photo of each face.
Then he downloads the photos onto his laptop.*

*On the laptop, in Photoshop, Mark begins gradually to align
each facial image with the others, flipping, resizing, layering,
blending and combining them to form one composite face.*

*He pauses. He looks at the result. Then he places the necklace
next to the laptop and tries to arrange it appropriately.*

*He unwraps the prepared canvas he bought and sets it on the easel,
arranging the laptop so that he can see the composite image.
He picks up the palette and brushes.
Looks at laptop and the necklace.
And pauses.*

33. INT. NOAH'S DINING ROOM.

*Noè is not quite completely drunk.
A splendid if somewhat chaotic spread of cold foods, but no meat,
is on the table, with several half empty wine bottles.
Mark deliberately drinks mainly water and very little wine.*

> NOÈ
> So you saw the Sistine Chapel today. It is quite
> good, isn't it. I've visited it a few times since it was
> finished. I'm always impressed. And I do like his
> little joke at my expense.

> MARK
> I'm not sure I saw the joke, Noè.

NOÈ

Julius was pretty annoyed, of course, as always.
He complained that Michelangelo had the whole
of divine and human history to choose from,
and he gives three of the nine central panels
to his mate, Noè—one of them shows me drunk as
a lord. Of course he'd seen me that way many
times—we used to drink together in the old
Il Segno dell' Arcobaleno—I had one just down
the road from the Vatican in those days—they were
good days, for a while. Thirsty work building that
dome. But they made me move to the ghetto later.
Not much business there. Never liked kosher.

MARK

So Michelangelo didn't paint you drunk
just because it's in the Bible?

NOÈ *(laughs)*

—*and* he goes and paints all those roaring nudes
all over the ceiling, every man jack of them showing
his all—well, until some of the cardinals had them
covered up a little—but then he paints the story
of me showing my bits and my sons being so
ashamed they have to cover me up. I ask you!
As if the world hadn't seen those nudes all over the
ceiling anyway. So, what else did you like, Mark?

MARK

Most of the place was closed. I saw the collection of
model boats, though—I don't suppose—

NOÈ

No, no, good guess, but the ark isn't amongst them.
Though they *were* looking for it. Right under their
noses, really. When I first landed here,
you could still get up the Tiber from Ostia.
You can't these days, too many bridges. Problem
getting it out again, too. Still, I did once agree to
have a model made, for Santa Maria di Dominica—

they asked me very nicely. It's still there, in stone,
but knocked about a bit.

MARK
Angelina tells me you nearly bought my Galileo icon
— but you thought he looked too old.
Did you know Galileo then?

NOÈ
Oh no, not well, not well at all. Used to drink with
Sagredo a lot, though. He kept me in touch with
all the Galileo gossip. Knew his daughter slightly.
It was she who told me that print you copied was
a bit unflattering. They always tried to make him out
to be some kind of shattered tragic figure—but he
quite enjoyed those last years, under house arrest.
Easy life for a glutton, after all, no money worries,
no need to keep inventing, or even teaching.
Though he did get on with a bit of work anyway.
He happily put on weight and looked well,
right to the end. So she said.

MARK
Noè, you are making all this up, aren't you?
I'm finding it a bit hard going.

NOÈ
Have another glass of wine, dear boy.
Much easier to believe things when you're, well,
happy. Not that I'm happy myself, you know.
That's why I drink. Well, I enjoy it too.
But I think it's coming, again.

MARK
What's coming again, Noè? The Flood.

NOÈ

Of course not. A promise is a promise, after all.
But I did think I'd be needed again, some time.
I was right. That's why I've been storing all these
things. The books, two copies of each. And the
paintings, two copies when I could get them.
But some people wouldn't play ball—or couldn't—
Picasso could never do the same painting twice.
He tried sometimes but they always turned out
differently. So I settled for just two Picassos.
Good ones though. I did try to get the best. *(pause)*
But I really can't see the point any more.
Why save them now? Nobody really cares about
books or paintings these days. They're just trophies.
Dead. In private collections. Or museums and
galleries. Just a tourist attraction. And the books are
all being, what do they call it, 'digitized'.
Who wants to read pages on a plastic screen?
Printing was bad enough. No more lovely painted
manuscripts. Anyway, none of this stuff will survive.
The fire next time. So he said. *(pause)* Global
warming. I'm just sorry for the animals. They
haven't a chance this time. I'm tired. Very tired.

MARK *(gently)*

Perhaps you should sleep it off, Noè. I have a lot
of work to do. Should I see you to bed first?

NOÈ

I'll be fine, young Mark. I can sleep anywhere.
Just pass me that other bottle.

Noè slumps to the floor and passes out.

*Mark cautiously puts a cushion under Noè's head,
waits a moment, then leaves quietly.*

34. INT. CORRIDOR.

Mark opens a door and looks in.
In the gloom he sees a clutter of obscure objects.
In one corner is a large seven-branched candlestick, covered in cobwebs.
Mark is about to take a photo, then shrugs and turns away,
goes along the corridor to the stairs, and heads upwards.

35. INT. ATTIC STUDIO IN NOAH'S HOUSE.
VERY EARLY LIGHT.

Mark works steadily at the portrait on the canvas which is now taking
shape. He is painting using the laptop composite image as his model.

He is still bothered by the problem of arranging the necklace.
Finally he puts the necklace in his pocket.

36. INT. DINING ROOM.

Mark leaves a pot of coffee, a cup, and a note by the sleeeping Noè.
The note reads: ' No Peeping! ' *Mark leaves quietly.*

37. INT. POLICE OFFICE.

A small office filled with filing cabinets and bookcases, with reports,
files and papers everywhere, but very orderly. On the desk is a large
computer and monitor.
Seated at the desk is Detective Inspector Zoretti, forty-odd, bright,
alert. He speaks slowly and deliberately, in careful English.
Mark has just entered. They shake hands. Mark sits.

> ZORETTI
> Thank you for coming, Mr Ferry. I hope
> you are enjoying your visit to Rome, despite
> this unfortunate business of your work being,
> shall we say, mislaid.

MARK

Mislaid? I thought they were stolen, Inspector.
Do you have any reason to think otherwise?

ZORETTI

Let me be plain speaking. I am not, of course,
accusing you, Mr Ferry—but shall we say that the
art dealer who so kindly sponsored your exhibition,
and who so carefully insured it also, is quite well
known to us. And we know that he has recently
suffered, shall we say, a bad loss—he invested
heavily in an Andy Warhol speculation. Always a
gamble, in my view. And the objects in question
proved to be, well, not entirely a reliable risk.
Soap boxes are not always signed, after all.
So, he needs to balance his books again, and we
believe he is trying in several small ways to recoup
his outgoings. So—let me put it this way:
if the insurance money for your exhibition is not
forthcoming, your work may possibly re-appear,
after all—or, of course, it may simply disappear
for good. A loss written off. But now that Signor
Bertolli believes, so I hear, that you are perhaps a
more profitable opportunity than he had thought,
I have little doubt that he will 'find' your work,
somehow. So may perhaps I suggest that you
remain patient. Time will tell.

MARK

So is that why you wanted to see me?
To tell me I'm just part of an art dealer scam?
I'm not sure I'm flattered.

ZORETTI

You have my sympathy, Signor Ferry. *(pause)*
But there was in fact another reason for my wishing
to see you. I hear that you are acquainted with
a Signor Noè, is that so?

MARK
Well, I am staying with him while I finish a painting
he has commissioned from me. Do you think he
was somehow implicated in this insurance scam?
I don't see how.

ZORETTI
No, no, not at all, Mr Ferry. And I would myself
not normally take an interest in such a minor
matter. Yes, minor, I'm afraid, though that may
offend you. You see, my department concerns itself
with somewhat larger issues. *(pause)*
May I ask if you have perhaps come across any
interesting works of art in Signor Noè's house?

MARK *(pause)*
May I ask why you wish to know, Inspector Zoretti?

ZORETTI
*(pauses for a moment, then reaches for a large volume on the
shelf behind him)* To see if anything Signor Noè
currently has in his possession might perhaps
match any of these —

*Zoretti flips open the large volume, which is a catalogue of art works,
with mainly small black and white illustrations alongside a long list of
individual works.*
Zoretti places the open volume in front of Mark. Mark looks at it.

MARK
What exactly am I looking at? Or what are you
looking *for*, Inspector?

ZORETTI
That is a version of the standard work by Herr
Klaus Rogner: *Verlorene Werke der Malerei in
Deutschland in der Zeit von 1939 bis 1945: Zerstörte und
Verschollene Gemälde aus Museen und Galerien.*

MARK
Meaning—?

ZORETTI
Lost works of painting in Germany in the period
from 1939 to 1945 : destroyed and missing paintings
from museums and galleries. In other words,
a list of Nazi plunder. I would also want you to
check against this website.

Zoretti swivels his computer screen to Mark.
It shows the following website: http://www.lootedart.com/search2.php

ZORETTI
As you can see, Mr Ferry, this is the website of the
Central Registry of Information on Looted
Cultural Property 1933 to 1945.

MARK
Are you telling me you think Signor Noè
is a Nazi art thief, a war criminal? That's absurd!

ZORETTI
Yes, it would be absurd, would it not.
If only because Signor Noè is a Jew. *(pauses)*
Let me tell you, Mr Ferry, the story of Signor Noè,
or rather of Signor David Lev Rabinovich.
It is quite moving, in its way.
(Zerotti settles into his chair and speaks slowly).
Let me call him simply David. *(pause)*
We know that David was born in May 1945,
in the very last chaotic days of the concentration
camp at Matthausen. That he was born at all in that
camp, or that he survived, is surely a miracle.
But he did survive, as an orphan. We know that he
was in a Vienna orphanage, in the Soviet sector,
until 1954. But his early life story is full of gaps.

Later, we know he lived on the streets, and in his teens he spent much time in the great museums and art galleries of Vienna—because, as he once said, they were so much warmer than the streets. The street urchin became well known to some of those museum officials and curators. The young David was street-wise, sharp, very bright, picked up languages easily, and had an extraordinary visual memory. In 1962, one of those sympathetic curators recommended David for a lowly office job in the Vienna section of the World Jewish Congress's Commission for Art Recovery.

And David discovered his vocation, his life's work. Over the next thirty years David Rabinovich became one of the most brilliant and dedicated investigators and pursuers of the missing looted art of Europe. He was credited with some of the more spectacular cases. In particular, he developed a passion for tracking down works which had been designated for Hitler's secret scheme for Linz, Hitler's own birthplace. The Matthausen camp, David's hellish birth-place, was only twenty kilometers from Linz. But Hitler had ordered the looting of so many works of art which he then rejected, as not suitable for his own narrow-minded and petit-bourgeois art tastes for Linz, that much of that work simply disappeared, mainly into the private collections of Nazi party members and their wealthy supporters. After the war, the legal case for proving any such works had been looted rather than, say, bought in a forced but legal sale was often difficult. *(pause)* So David developed, shall we say, a certain specialism. He would track down a work or a collection where the current alleged owners would be very reluctant indeed to see their ownership made public, still less their claims tested in open court—and then somehow that work or collection would simply disappear from their possession —

MARK
You're saying that Noè, or David, *stole* them back?

ZORETTI
Yes. That is indeed what we think. But from the
nature of such cases, it is obviously difficult to
prove. Often, such works would mysteriously
reappear, now as the property of the State of Israel,
or be assigned by an Israeli judicial commission to
some museum or even a private owner once again.
(pause) But then things changed drastically
for David Rabinovich. He had married in 1976
and by the late 1990s the couple had two grown-up
sons, both working in Israel. In July 1997, David's
older son was killed in a Hamas suicide bomb in the
Jerusalem market. A year later, his younger son was
shot dead when Israeli forces opened fire on a
pro-Palestinian solidarity demonstration. *(pause)*
David's wife, Nina, died shortly after. She may have
committed suicide. David was utterly broken.
He resigned from the Art Recovery Commission
and became a recluse. He seems to have suffered
a very long depression. *(pause)* When he re-emerged,
it was as Signor Noè. And it was then, we think,
that he, shall we say, went into business for himself.
(pause) By then, of course, he knew not only the
entire legitimate art market across Europe but also
most of the professional art thieves and fences.
And concerning most of the art dealers in Europe,
legitimate and otherwise, David held, shall we say,
interesting information about the provenance of
some of their past dealings. But he no longer
handed over to Israel any art works he obtained.
By then David had lost faith in Israel. When an
American legal suit was filed to claim and sell
Persian antiquities held in American museums,
as financial recompense for Israeli victims of a
Hamas massacre, for which the American courts
somehow held Iran responsible, he publicly
opposed it. And then he financed a counter-suit

to claim Israeli assets held in the the USA as
damages for the Israeli blockade of Gaza.
More recently he publicly denounced Israel's claim
to ownership of the papers of Franz Kafka—that
claim is on the curious grounds that all orphaned
Jewish cultural artefacts somehow now belong to
the State of Israel. A claim perhaps relevant also
to all the lost art works of the Nazi period.
So you will not be surprised that the Israelis,
like us, are most interested in David's, shall we say,
continuing activities.

MARK
Why on earth does Noè think, er, why does
David call himself Noè?

ZORETTI
Frankly, Mr Ferry, we regard David Rabinovich as
now somewhat insane. Unhinged. Unfortunately,
when he was recovering from his deep depression,
it seems that he read a novel by a compatriot of
yours, a writer called Alan Wall. The novel was
The Book of Noah and concerned a man who
thought he was Noah and had lived for thousands
of years, running a little bar or inn in various
significant places and times in European history,
and getting to know all sorts of famous people.
It is a very good and very interesting novel.
But David sadly identified himself as the Noah
of that very work of fiction. And now he lives
in a complete fantasy world.
As Noah. Survivor of the Flood. *(pause)*
But perhaps his collection of art works, stolen and
then re-stolen, is not, we think, a fantasy.
As yet, we have no proof. We have tried to obtain a
legal search warrant—but David knows enough
about several major art collections and where they
once came from, including some in Italy

and some in Israel itself, that our own authorities
and even the Israelis are not, it would appear,
at all keen to see him in court, for any reason.
And other methods of, shall we say, investigating
his works have not been very successful.
David has learned much from his own victims,
and his vast house is now extremely well protected,
almost a fortress—unless, of course, he opens the
door himself. Which he only very rarely does.
And certainly not to us. Though he did to you,
for some reason. *(pause)* The Israelis are, we think,
content to wait until he dies. Nobody really wants to
hurt an unhinged old man. But my job is still to find
out where nearly 16,000 missing works of art are.
And perhaps Signor Noè has a few?

>   MARK
In that novel, would Noè's inn have been called
'The Sign of the Rainbow', by any chance?

>   ZORETTI
Indeed it was. Now, Mr Ferry, would you care
to help us?

>   MARK
Well, I have seen some rather old books
in his library. He does have a very large library.
Does that help?

>   ZORETTI
It might. Books, of course, are not unique,
as a painting is. That you have a particular printed
book doesn't prove you stole that copy, unless it is
inscribed or otherwise identifiable. But, yes, one of
the last official cases David Rabinovich was
involved in concerned a certain well-known
professor in Munich, who had an entire apartment
full of very rare and extremely valuable books.

Which he was somehow unable to explain how he obtained. That collection was eventually donated, quite freely, of course, to the Hebrew University— though some books never quite reached Jerusalem —a first folio Shakespeare, for example, was in the inventory but had disappeared. And David Rabinovich was always very interested in what had happened to the very fine libraries of the old Rome Synagogues and of the Rabbinical College here — they were 'taken into safe keeping' in 1943 and have not been since since, though a few books were saved. *(pauses)* Would you like some time to think further, Mr Ferry? You will not be leaving Rome shortly, I hope.

            MARK
Well, I do have a painting to finish first.
And right now, I have a young lady to meet,
if you will excuse me—

            ZORETTI
Certainly. You have been most helpful.
Perhaps if you were able to, shall we say, take some
photographs, it would be even more helpful.
I hope to see you again, Mr Ferry— as I hope you
will soon see your own work again. Arrivederci.

38. EXT. OUTSIDE TEATRO DINONA.

Mark and Angelina meet, with a warm exchange of cheek kisses.

            ANGELINA
How did it go?

            MARK
It left me a lot to think about. Forgive me,
Angelina, if I'm a bit preoccupied. But basically,
Zerotti thinks Bertolli 'stole' my work to get the
insurance, and that it will somehow just turn up.

So the advice is to wait and see. Not very satisfying.
But not much I can do either. I can hardly accuse
him outright. But, now, where is it we're going?

ANGELINA
To the Basilica of San Clemente.
Let me tell you why—it's a good story.

39. INTERIOR. SAN CLEMENTE.

*An extended sequence of shots of Mark and Angelina gradually
making their way right down into the various layers of San Clemente:
the fourth century basilica beneath the 12th century church, then the
second century Mithraic Temple beneath the fourth century structures,
and finally the 1st century A.D. house complex.*

40. EXTERIOR. CLOISTER OF SAN CLEMENTE.
BRIGHT SUNSHINE.

*Mark and Angelina are standing at the display diagram in the corner
of the cloister. Mark is moving the superimposed diagrams of the
various archaeological layers over each other, still making sense of it*

MARK
That was just amazing. I can't get over it.
You never know what you're going to find
when you start digging!

ANGELINA
In Rome, yes. But even in Rome San Clemente is
exceptional. To have so many layers so accessible.
And you still haven't really looked at the present
church. Remember even today there are Byzantine
mosaics and 14th century frescoes on 12th century
walls. Layer on layer.

MARK
Give me time to recover. I'm still in the fourth
century, or the second, or the first.
With Mithraic worshippers, and Nero's burning
Rome. You could still see the scorch marks—
and that snake altar. Extraordinary.

ANGELINA *(smiles at him)*
Go and refresh your mind with the beautiful
Saint Catherine—shouldn't she be one of your
science icons, an intelligent woman arguing with
the false beliefs of her own day? She's on the wall of
the chapel, just to the left of the entrance, complete
with her wheel. I'm going to stay out here.

Angelina sits on a bench at the side of the cloister.
Mark goes into the church.

41. EXT. CLOISTER OF SAN CLEMENTE.
BRIGHT SUNSHINE.

Angelina is dozing in the sun.
Her mobile phone rings. She answers it and listens.

ANGELINA
Sì, lo so, non ha mai'il telefono acceso.*(a very long*
pause while she listens intently). Gli dirò. Ciao.

She waits and thinks.

42. EXT. CLOISTER OF SAN CLEMENTE.
BRIGHT SUNSHINE.

Mark comes over from the church and sits comfortably beside Angelina.

MARK
They were good. Very good. But I'm still
somewhere underground, I think. *(pause)*
You look concerned about something?

ANGELINA

Bertolli just rang. Your Inspector was apparently
right. Bertolli claims that he was so angry about
Donizone that immediately after that meeting
yesterday, he put out a big reward to get the works
back. And put the word around all the dealers
he knows. And so on. Any rate, his story is that
the works have now turned up—and he wants to do
another exhibition of your work, immediately.
To cash in on the scandal, the publicity, he says.

MARK

(ironic laugh) What a surprise, eh— But I don't
understand the bit about 'the scandal, publicity'.
What does he mean?

ANGELINA

Well, he partly means the scandal around the
demonstrations against the Galileo play last week.
Remember I said it was on the news channels and
so on. But that's last week's news. There's also been
a further development. And this is the bit you won't
like. *(pause)* Your works have all been recovered, he
says—but they've all been defaced.

MARK

What!?

ANGELINA

He says those Christian fundamentalists were
obviously responsible, since each work now has
stencilled across it quotations from the bible,
about graven images, and crosses in red paint
have been painted onto the faces of the scientists,
with slogans like 'God alone is Truth', 'I am the
way, the truth and the life' and so on, daubed all
over them. They're ruined—but, claims Bertolli,
that makes them even *more* saleable.

An instant art scandal—just the kind of thing that
sells art these days, he says. So he's busy generating
as much instant publicity as he can, and wants
the new opening at his gallery tomorrow night.
He also wants the three new works you brought
with you to include in the show. And will you
ring him immediately.

Angelina hands him her phone.

> MARK
> Wait, wait, wait. Hang on. I need to think. *(pause)*
> Did he say anything else?

> ANGELINA
> Quite a lot. He says his wealthy clients will pay very
> good money for a good story to hang on the wall.
> So long as they don't need to say anything about the
> actual art, but can just tell the tale of how they were
> stolen and defaced by some lunatic fundamentalists
> in a famous scandal—So he's going to price them at
> five thousand euros each. The gallery takes 50 per
> cent. And he claims he still has the right to show
> and sell them till the end of this week anyway,
> whether you approve or not. The original contract
> for the theatre exhibition is still in force.

> MARK
> The scheming bastard. Right. I'll ring him.

Mark takes the phone and then hesitates, uncertain.
Angelina smiles, takes it back from him and presses the right button,
then hands it back.

> MARK
> *(firmly)* Signor Bertolli, Mark Ferry here —
> *(he is clearly interrupted, and then tries to get a word in)*
> I don't think —that's not how I — I don't —
> You will what? —*(finally pauses and listens. Long pause.*

Then:) Look, Bertolli, I don't give a damn about
your contract. But I will, as you say, have to honour
it. But on one condition—No, I will not interfere
with the hanging of the show. You say you know
what you're doing, you're the professional—yes.
You know your market. I hear all that. Now look,
I don't even want to see my work before
tomorrow night. You describe the state of it
very clearly, thank you. But I am telling you to
leave a clear wall space for one more portrait
to hang. —Yes, a new one. Standard A3, 420 by 300
mill. Unframed. I want it prominent. By itself.
Clear? Yes? *(pause)* Agreed. Yes, you can have the
other three new ones later today. Send someone
to pick them up from Signor Noè's. At about seven
tonight. And I'll bring the other new one and hang
it myself tomorrow. At the opening. It's at eight-
thirty? Right. I will see you there.

Mark looks at Angelina. He looks furious.

                    MARK
The—come dice?—thieving scheming nasty
money-grubbing little bastard!

Then they both burst out laughing. She hugs him.

                    MARK
He's got me over a barrel. But I'm going to get
one small piece of satisfaction out of it all.
I'm quite proud of the painting I've just been doing
for old Noè. And I hope he will be too. So I'm
planning that it will simply upstage all the other
work and that it will give Noè some pleasure to see
it as the centre-piece of the exhibition. *If* he'll
come to the opening. If he won't, I'll just leave a
blank on the wall. Which reminds me —

Mark fishes in his pocket and brings out the ancient pearl necklace,
covered in tissue paper. Hands it to Angelina, who opens
the tissue paper and does a double-take of surprise and pleasure.

MARK
Now, will you put that on for me.

ANGELINA
Delighted! It's absolutely lovely, Mark.
You really shouldn't —

MARK *(highly embarrassed)*
Ah! No. Sorry. I didn't mean it that way. I just want
you to *model* it for me, so I can take a photo
and get the way it hangs right on your neck.
I'm sorry. Maybe with my fifty per cent of sales
I can buy you another one.

Angelina blows him a kiss and puts the necklace on.
He takes several photos as she poses.
Then takes the necklace back and puts it away.

ANGELINA
Well, at least you promised me dinner tonight.

MARK
Oh my God, yes. I did, didn't I. Erm, can we make
it tomorrow. Please. If I'm going to finish this
painting now in time for tomorrow, I need all the
light I can get—all this afternoon, and then I'll have
to get up at the crack of dawn tomorrow,
then hopefully leave it time to dry enough by
tomorrow evening. Erm, how about tomorrow—
lunch, afternoon tea, er, breakfast?

ANGELINA
I see. First you fob me off with a temporary
necklace, and now just 'afternoon tea' tomorrow.

(laughs) But you're going to be free all day
tomorrow, after your dawn labours have finished?
So, where else in Rome do you want to go to?
I shall be your faithful guide, despite your appalling
behaviour to me.

Mark tries to embrace her—but she fends him off playfully.

ANGELINA
Not in a church cloister, young sir.

MARK
Actually, there is something I'd love to do
tomorrow. I'd been thinking about it before I came.
But it's not in Rome. Ever since a friend of mine
described it, I've been wanting to see the Cinque
Terre. He said the coastline there was simply
stunningly beautiful. I'd worked out it's possible to
get a train up there and back in a few hours, and
that was something I'd promised myself on this trip.
Is that possible? And would you like that?

ANGELINA
Yes, I would. I know that coast well, and, yes,
the road is wonderful. But it's actually too far to
drive and back. The fast train should be possible,
yes, but it must be an early start if we're to be back
in time for the opening.

MARK
It will take my mind off it all, and at least it won't
involve any more walking around Rome. I need new
feet after only two days.

ANGELINA
Weakling. Alright. I'll check train times and come
to Noè's early, say 6 a.m. Will that give you enough
hours of proper morning light. Yes?

MARK

Yes, I think so. I know exactly what I still
need to do. If I get to Noè's now. Pronto. Yes?

43. INT. ATTIC STUDIO.

*Mark adds the photos of Angelina wearing the necklace to the laptop
and again composites the layered images of faces in Photoshop,
with her face now prominently as the top layer.*
*He turns back to the painting and begins to work rapidly on it,
smiling and humming happily to himself*

44. INT. DINING ROOM. LATE EVENING.

*There is a meal, again cold, vegetables, bread, fruit, cheese.
Some open bottles. Noè is fairly sober. Mark is eating hungrily.
The conversation drifts amicably.*

NOÈ

You say it is nearly finished, Mark.
That is remarkably fast.

MARK

The way I work, with composited digital scans,
it's qiite easy to compress the process. And I'm
using the modern kinds of quick-drying paints
I told you about.

NOE

So may I look at it tomorrow, while you are out
with Angelina? I would rather like to see it
before this exhibition in the evening.

MARK

Of course, Signor Noè. It is your painting after all.
I'm only too pleased that you agreed to allow it to
be in the exhibition at all. And that you've agreed
to come to the opening.

NOÈ
Do call me Noè. Or Noah. You find it easier,
I know.

MARK
Thank you, Noè. Noah. Er, do you have
a first name?

NOÈ
God did not give me one, I'm glad to say.

(Pause)

MARK *(very cautiously)*
Noè, did you ever hear of an English writer,
called Alan Wall?

NOÈ
Ah, yes, young Alan. I do remember.
He came and interviewed me some years ago.
I told him my life story, as I have told you, in part.
I remember he was most interested in my stay
in Vienna just before the last war. No, sorry, not the
last one. The one we used to call The Great War.
Though there was nothing great about it.
Or any war. I recall Karl Kraus used to call it
the Last Days of Mankind.
He was nearly right. As so often.

MARK
You were in Vienna, then?

NOÈ
Yes, for a while. I told Alan I tried to take treatment
for my bad dreams with Herr Doktor Freud.
But it was not a success. He said my dreams were
telling me the truth. Whatever that was.
I told him he was mistaken about what he called
'the Unconscious'. The unconscious is simply what
we cannot face, cannot bring to consciousness.

It's not some entity inside us. I had to correct
Paul the tent-maker in much the same way.
He thought the Greeks in Athens had a statue
'To The Unknown God'. I told him the Greek
inscription just meant that they didn't know *which*
God it was a statue of, simply an unidentified statue,
not some great Unknown Deity.

MARK *(gently)*
May I ask when you were born, Noè?
Do you remember?

NOÈ
Does anybody remember their birth? We just
believe what we are told. I could be any age.

MARK *(very gently)*
I spoke to a police inspector today, Noè.
He claims your birth certificate says you were born
in a concentration camp. In 1945.

NOÈ
We are all born in a concentration camp, Mark.
Not a garden. It has not got any better. *(pause)*
I know what you're saying, my dear Mark. I know
that Inspector Zoretti thinks I'm crazy, unbalanced.
Well, what could be easier to forge than
a birth certificate from a concentration camp?
Just a scribble on a scrap of paper. Who really kept
records of births, even of deaths, there, then?
I needed an identity, yet again. It was convenient.
I didn't think it would cause too many problems.

MARK
And are you Jewish, Noè?

NOÈ

Of course not. The Jews came later,
with their 'covenant'. There were no Jews or
Israelites before that. I was the father, the second
father, of *all* mankind, not just of the Jews,
you know. And I have watched all my sons and
daughters slaughter each other ever since.

MARK

So you think you really are Noah?
How do you know? *(pause)* I remember, as a very
small boy, being introduced to a very very old man.
(smiles) I asked him: 'Were you in the ark?'
He laughed and said he hadn't been.
Then I asked him: 'So why weren't you drowned? '
He laughed, a lot, at that.

NOÈ *(laughs)*

I like that. Well, birth certificates. Passports.
Identity cards. Getting new ones made. Again.
That was the problem with my lovely wife, Neemah.
She never aged, always remained so beautiful.
I did, slowly, look a bit older, and then even older,
myself, as the years went by. But she was still young.
Radiant. So people used to ask awkward questions,
after a while. If we stayed in one place for more
than fifty years, they got very suspicious,
thought she was a witch, or something like that.
So we would have to move on, lose ourselves
and appear in a new place, open yet another bar
or a little café, or a hotel, and again the local artists
would come flocking. They all fell in love with her,
of course. And we told fine stories too. Always
good for business. But this last century or so,
it's become so much harder to move on, to lose
yourself, to start again. Everybody has to have
papers, passports, identity cards, bank accounts, e-
mail addresses, phone numbers. It's not my world.
Or hers. *(pause)*

One day, I woke up and she had gone.
And I couldn't find her. She didn't have any
up-to-date papers, you see. That's when I invented
mine, my holocaust survivor identity.
So she could find me. If she wanted to.
When I saw your Hypatia, I thought: that looks
so much like her, maybe she's been his model,
as in the old days, so maybe I can contact her
through him. But you didn't know her, after all.

> MARK

I'm sorry, Noè. *(pause)* Now I must get to bed early,
so I can get up with the dawn and finish the last
touches on her portrait. If the exhibition gets the
kind of publicity Signor Berolli is planning,
perhaps she'll hear about it, even see her portrait
in the newspapers, or on the net. You never know.
Good night, Noah.

> NOÈ

Good night, Mark. Sleep well.

> MARK

And you, Noah.

45. INT. ATTIC STUDIO. VERY EARLY MORNING.

Mark is putting the finishing touches to the portrait. He is pleased.

46. EXT. STREET NEAR TERMINI STATION.
EARLY MORNING.

Mark and Angelina are running towards the station, breathless but laughing.

Sudddenly Mark stops. He goes back a few paces, to an old woman, semi-blind, who is sitting on a doorstep, and is trying to retrieve a slipper with her white stick.

He kneels down, gets the slipper and puts it on her foot.
Then he straightens up and races to catch up with Angelina,
who has stopped to watch.

47. PLATFORM. TERMINI STATION.

Mark and Angelina pile onto a train.

48. INSIDE MOVING TRAIN CARRIAGE.

Mark and Angelina are seated in a corner of the carriage,
facing forward, on the right.

Across the aisle is a large window and no seating.
They have almost panoramic views.

Mark has his head nestling on Angelina and he is fast asleep.
She is amused.

49. INSIDE TRAIN CARRIAGE.

Angelina shakes Mark groggily awake.

> ANGELINA
> Mark, you've been asleep for more than two hours.
> Fine date this is! *(she smiles at him)* We're coming
> towards the first of the Cinque Terre.
> This is what you wanted to see, isn't it?

> MARK
> Mmm. Tired. Wanna sleep.*(he shakes himself out of it)*
> Right, I am alert, awake, watchful. Alive!
> And in love with a beautiful woman.

> ANGELINA
> You're still dreaming. Pay attention to the scenery.
> Here's Viareggio.

As the train approaches the spectacular Viareggio coastline,
a young couple with a baby in a carry-cot come down the carriage,
to get off at the station. They stop in the passageway, just in front of
Mark and Angelina. Three teenage girls come behind the couple
and they all crowd round the baby, making coo-ing noises, etc.

They completely block Mark's view of the coastline
until the train pulls into the station. They get off.

But all Mark can now see is the station platform. He looks rueful.

The train pulls out of the station and almost immediately goes into a
tunnel. There are only a few fleeting glimpses of the sea
through brief openings.

50. INSIDE TRAIN CARRIAGE.

The train is beginning to slow down.

> ANGELINA
> Masso Centro. We should be out of this tunnel —
> soon.

A hugely fat man comes down the carriage and parks himself
at the window on the coast side. He has his back to the window
and is eating his way through a large slice of pizza.

As the coastline becomes visible he stays there, almost entirely blocking
the view.

Mark and Angelina can again see nothing of the view—
and start to giggle.

51. INSIDE TRAIN CARRIAGE.

The train is back in a series of tunnels with just intermittent
and very brief glimpses of the sea.

ANGELINA
(*trying not to laugh*) Now, La Spezia is *really* beautiful.

*As the train clears the tunnel and the coastline is briefly visible,
another train arrives on the inside, track and blocks their view
completely. No sea or coast is visible at all.*

MARK
I give up. Where do we get off?

ANGELINA
(*she laughs*) I bought return tickets to Rapallo.
I remembered going to Rapallo, as a child.
We went there one winter. There was a marvellous
Funivia up the mountain. But it was closed.

MARK
Chiusa.

52. EXT. RAPALLO. AT THE FUNIVIA STATION.

*The ticket window is closed. The funicular carriage is empty and
deserted. A large sign says: 'CHIUSA : 12.30—14.00.'
Mark and Angelina are looking at it. Angelina looks at her watch.*

ANGELINA
It's 12.35 now And we have to get the train back
at 13.40.

MARK
AAAgh!

*They burst out laughing.
A young girl appears from the door of the ticket office.*

GIRL
Vuoi ascendere? C'è un matrimonio alla chiesa di
oggi, perciò lavoriamo durante l'ora di pranzo.

ANGELINA
Si, si! *(to Mark, happily)* There's a wedding
at the church at the top, so they're running
the funivia. We can go up now.

MARK
Thank God for weddings!

53. EXT. ON MONTALLEGRO.

*Mark and Angelina are standing side by side
looking at the stupendous view, with the white church behind them.
They are eating ice creams. They turn to face each other
and Mark tries to kiss Angelina on the lips, only to get his and her
ice-cream smeared all over their faces. They burst out laughing.*

54. EXT. CAFE OUTSIDE RAPALLO STATION.

*Mark and Angelina are having coffees, waiting for their train.
Angelina picks up an abandoned copy of the Rome edition of La
Repubblica from another table and leafs through it. Suddenly stops.*

ANGELINA
Well, Bertolli has done it. 'Publicity', he said.

She points to an inside article in the newspaper.

ANGELINA *(reads and translates:)*
'The trials of Galileo, still! Opening at the Bertolli
Gallery this evening will be an exhibition of works
by the English artist Mark Ferry which were stolen
by Christian fundamentalists last week. Ferry's
work on the images of science, featuring portraits of
famous scientists such as Galileo and Newton, had
been on show to accompany the production by
Teatrodinona of Bertolt Brecht's play on Galileo
which was controversially picketted and forced to
close. After Bertolli's offered a substantial reward,

the works were recovered but they had all been
scandalously defaced with anti-science slogans.
The defaced works will go on show and on sale
as a gesture of defiance to such reactionary attacks.
The Rome cultural community sees in this case yet
another assault on progressive artists and on
modern science by a reactionary movement
which the Vatican has so far refused to condemn.
A spokesman for the Vatican said they had
no comment on this latest developments in the
ongoing battle between religious beliefs and science.
The Bertolli Gallery has issued a statement urging
all those who are prepared to stand up for modern
progressive values to support the new exhibition'
blah, blah, blah.

                    MARK
That's nearly spoilt my day—but not quite.

He leans over to kiss her properly. And succeeds.
The sun beams down happily, of course.

55. BERTOLLI GALLERY. EVENING.

The gallery is very chic and fairly full of an expensively-dressed
clientele, chattering and drinking. Around the walls are Mark's
defaced works, some of which are already marked with a red dot to
indicate a sale. Bertolli is in the crowd, visibly pleased with himself.

Mark, Angelina and Noah arrive at the door.
Noah is in very *old-fashioned evening dress and is fairly sober.*
Mark is carrying a portfolio.
Angelina has changed into an evening dress and looks ravishing.

Mark goes into the gallery space, looks around,
and then finds the vacant space on the wall.

He takes the new portrait out of the portfolio and starts to hang it.
Bertolli spots him and comes over.
Mark carries on adjusting the hanging.

BERTOLLI
Mark, you've arrived. I was beginning to wonder.
(looks at the portrait). That *is* good. My word.
But you say it's not for sale? Pity. *(spots Noè)*
Ah, Signor Noè. I must congratulate you on your
choice of artist. May I get you a drink?

NOÈ
No thank you. I'm here to admire and I can
best do that sober.

BERTOLLI
Mark, a drink? And then I might say a few words,
introduce you, usual spiel, you know. We've sold
five already. Going to be a very good evening.

Mark has been looking around the gallery at the rest of the exhibition.
He is clearly angry.

MARK
Bertolli, we need a word.

BERTOLLI
Certainly, Mark. In my office. But in a moment.
First, *(he taps his glass and announces)* Signore e
signori, amici, ammiratori d'arte, il nostro artista
è arrivato, finalmente. Un applauso per lui,
se non vi dispiace. Ma tutti discorsi più tardi.
Commercio prima, affari, affari, come sempre, i
miei amici! Torneremo presto.

There is a scattering of applause as Bertolli takes Mark into the office
at the back of the gallery.

Angelina looks at Noè and grimaces.

Suddenly, through the door comes Eamonn Boyle, the American
christian protestor from the Galileo demonstration footage.

He spots Noè in his evening dress and comes over and confronts him.

BOYLE

Are you the guy in charge here? Is this your gallery,
sir? Well, I demand an apology, sir. You have not
only mocked the Good Lord but you have accused
His people of thieving, of stealing. That is against
the Lord's commandments, sir, and *we* do *not* steal.
We do not steal, sir, and I demand that you
withdraw that accusation.

NOÈ *(very politely)*
And you are?

BOYLE

Eamonn Boyle is my name sir and I am a true God-
fearing christian who believes in the Word of God,
in every word of God, not the damnable mockery
of your art and your science. I am —

NOÈ *(interrupts him, very politely).*
I am *so* glad to hear that, my dear Mr Boyle.
You do indeed believe in every word of the good
Bible, do you, sir?

BOYLE *(taken aback)*
I do indeed, sir.

NOÈ

I wonder, then, my dear Mr Boyle, could you
resolve a little puzzle that has bothered me for a
very long time indeed. *(Noah takes him by the arm and
speaks earnestly and confidentially)* Now, I too wish to
obey the Lord in all things, to follow his commands,
his every word. But I have sometimes been
confused as to what precisely those commands are.

BOYLE

Well, sir, that is truly a problem we may all have
at some time or other. What, may I ask, concerns
you, Mr — er?

NOÈ

Well, it says in Genesis chapter six, verse nineteen:
'And of every living thing of all flesh, you shall
bring *two* of every sort into the ark, to keep them
alive with you; they shall be male and female.
Of the birds according to their kinds, and of the
animals according to their kinds, of every creeping
thing of the ground according to its kind, two of
every sort shall come in to you, to keep them alive. '
Now, is that not the very word of the Lord, Mr
Boyle?

BOYLE

That is so, sir. Yessir, indeed it is.
I am glad you know your Bible, Mr — er —

NOÈ

Yet, Mr Boyle, in the very next chapter, chapter
seven, verse two, the good God also said: '
Take with you *seven pairs* of all clean animals,
the male and his mate; and a pair of the animals that
are not clean, the male and his mate; and *seven pairs*
of the birds of the air also, male and female, to keep
their kind alive upon the face of all the earth. '
Now, I ask the Lord, and you, my dear sir, *which* is a
man to do? *Two* of each or *seven pairs* of each?
I have often wondered if I got it right, you see.

BOYLE *(a little flummoxed)*

Well, sir, these, er, minor details, these small
differences, should not worry us unduly —

NOÈ

It was *not* a minor detail, I do assure you, my dear
Mr Boyle. It made an enormous difference.
To the whole size of the ark. To the amount of
wood that was needed. And gopher wood was
not very easy to obtain in those days, let me tell you.
As for making decisions about the food storage
calculations—

56. INT. BERTOLLI'S OFFICE.

MARK *(angry)*

So you agree the whole thing is a scam, and you still
expect me to go out there and 'say a few words'.
What if I tell them you've admitted *you* stole
the works in the first place and that it was you who
did the defacing of them? Because you're going to
have a damn hard time explaining how the
three new works I only gave you yesterday have
somehow ended up also being defaced in exactly the
same way.

BERTOLLI *(unruffled)*

You have a lot to learn, young man, about your
chosen profession. I defaced them because at this
moment in time they are worth a helluva lot more
that way. Look, Mark, you have to take your
chance when you can get it. You're not all that
good an artist, are you, really, though I do think that
new portrait has maybe got something, yes.
But you are *now*, for just *a few moments*, for a week or
two maybe, a *fashionable* artist, talked about,
a name in the news. Thanks to *me*. You can *sell*.
And the true value of an artist isn't how 'good'
his work is but how much it sells for. You're a hot
property *right now*. Because your work has been
vandalised by some reactionary religious nut-cases.
And that makes you a celebrity. But give it a
month, and maybe some people will still have you

on their wall, in a guest room or wherever, and
they'll tell the story one more time. But by then
someone else will be having *their* fashionable
opening, again thanks to *me*. Unless you can come
up with a real winner again and again, a sure-fire
formula, you're going to be just another struggling
artist. So take the money now and keep your —

MARK
Bertolli, the only reason I'm not going out there
to blow you away is because I persuaded Noah to
come here and to see his wife's portrait on show
to lots of admiring people, and I'm not going to
spoil this evening for him. But the price of my
keeping quiet right now is this : that you announce
that *none* of my work is for sale. Is that clear.

BERTOLLI *(irritated)*
We've already sold five —

MARK
So, you made a mistake. You give the money back.
Tell them *all* the work was pre-sold by me, as a
collection, before the show. And no individual item
is now available. Either that, or I ring your
insurance man Donizone right now and
invite him here this evening.

BERTOLLI
You're a fool. *(pause)* But yes, I agree. You do know
you'll never have another exhibition in Rome.

MARK
Perhaps *you* won't. Now I'll tell you something.
Donizone is already here. I saw him in the crowd.

BERTOLLI
Merda.

57. INTERIOR. BERTOLLI GALLERY.

Noè is still holding Boyle by the arm and talking urgently to him.
Boyle looks very alarmed indeed.

> NOÈ
>
> You see, it was quite impossible to know what He
> was really thinking. Was the flood going to last
> forty days and forty nights, as he said at first.
> Or was it going to be a hundred and fifty days.
> Or maybe seven months. Or even ten. I tell you it's
> pretty frustrating, trying to work out conflicting
> messages like those. Especially if you have to stock
> up on animal feed. It lasted more than a year in the
> end. A lot longer than I'd planned for.
> We were all *very* hungry by then.

> BOYLE *(very flustered)*
>
> Well, sir, some people do say this is, er, a kind of an
> editorial problem. You see, they claim there was
> this Jah-whist chronicler and then a Priestly writer,
> and they kind of had different traditions, and,
> well, I don't buy it myself but I suppose —

> NOÈ
>
> Yes, that's another thing, you know. That Yahwist
> scribe wrote that: 'all the days of Noah were nine
> hundred and fifty years: and he died.' Well, he was
> wrong, wasn't he. The Priest got it sort of right,
> Genesis 5:24: 'he walked with God, and was not, for
> God took him. ' But even he got confused about
> *who* didn't die—thought it was grandfather Enoch.
> But do I look dead to you?

Bertolli interrupts by clinking on his glass for an announcement.
Boyle tries to take the chance to slip away, looking shaken.
Noè holds him firmly by the arm.

BERTOLLI
My friends, I'm afraid I have to confess to a little
mistake this evening. For which I apologise.
Mark tells me that in fact *all* the work on show
tonight has already been sold, to an anonymous
collector and that —

He is loudly interrupted by Noè, who comes forward, waving a glass.
He is now mildly drunk.

NOÈ
Anonymous, my eye, Bertolli! I don't mind people
knowing *I* agreed to buy them all. *Before* they were
damn well defaced too. But I don't mind that.
Just look at that portrait, ladies and gentlemen.
Wouldn't *you* be proud to have commissioned that?
I am. So, Bertolli, this is for the rest of Mark's work
—

Noè goes over to Bertolli and tries to put some money into his hand.
The money falls to the floor. It is several heavy old silver coins.
About thirty. Which roll around the floor under the feet of the crowd.
People scramble onto their knees to grab them as they roll. Chaos.

Noè goes to recapture Boyle, who is trying to leave rapidly.

58. INT. NOÈ'S DINING ROOM.

Mark, Angelina and Noè are at the table with full glasses and
a very old and dusty wine bottle open before them. They clink glasses.

NOÈ
I did enjoy that.

ANGELINA
Especially when Bertolli saw Donizone was there.
And Donizone told him there would be no
insurance money for the theft or the damage,
since it had actually put the prices up!

MARK

You were brilliant, Noah. I loved that speech you
finally gave about how nobody really cared about art
any more, they were just followers of fashion, and
Leonardo would have despised them all—how
dealers nowadays passed off any old scribble of his
as worth thousands. Bertolli was furious.

NOÈ

Well, I meant it. Your portrait of my Neemah
was the first really *alive* painting I've seen for years.
But most people can't tell the difference
between truth and technique.

MARK

They do go together, Noah.

NOÈ

I know that, young Mark. I've seen it happen.
But most of the time now I despair. It doesn't seem
that any art makes any difference to people any
more, except to their bank balances, their wallets.
I've stopped buying new work. Most of the work is
large in scale and tiny in talent. Designed to hang on
corporate walls. And I must be one of the few
people with walls big enough to hang the stuff on
in my own house. But it's either empty and bland,
or just childish ego, someone waving frantically
and shouting: 'It's Me. It's Me. I'm Different.'

ANGELINA

I disagree, Noè. Some art does make a difference.
Our theatre, for example. Putting on Brecht's play
has made people think—even when they didn't
come to it. The demonstrations against it made
people think as well. Art doesn't 'change things',
I accept, but it can change people, who can then
make a difference to the world.

NOÈ

Going to the theatre doesn't make people *think*.
They just talk about the actors or the set design
or the lighting. Or the last production they saw.
Or the next one they're going to.

MARK

That's unfair, Noah. Remember what you said
about that very first taste of coffee. Well, the *first*
time you see a great play, like *Galileo* or *Lear*, or
listen to Mozart's *Requiem*, it can be an incredible
experience. Your comment only applies, maybe,
to people hearing the Mozart *Requiem* for the
hundredth time. Or going to yet another exhibition
or concert because it's the fashionable thing to do.
It's not art that fails. It's people who fail to keep
that freshness of response. In that sense, Bertolli
was partly right: because my works had, they
thought, been vandalised, at least they had
to think about *why* and why it *mattered*.

NOÈ

Angelina, I'm afraid I still think of the theatre
as just another form of entertainment. It always has
been. The circus bit of bread and circuses.
When I lived in Pompeii there were three theatres,
and that's a lot for a pretty small town. All of them
put on shows which packed them in, sometimes
sea fights, sometimes spectacular dancing displays,
but most often gladiators—people hacking each
other to death while other people cheered them on.
(pauses) I had some good friends among those
gladiators. I used to supply the drinks to the shows,
and I would slip them a few flasks. When the
volcano started spewing that thick ash everywhere,
they were all left locked in their cells. In the
gladiator school. Fifty of them. Their guards had
fled. And I couldn't get the cell doors to open.

They knew they were all doomed. To a man,
they put on their fighting gear, their uniforms,
their whole array of armour and weapons.
And they stood to attention, waiting for the end.
They were *proud* of what they were.
I cried. But they were really just murderers.
For entertainment. People deceive themselves about
the arts they practise. Blood, sex, fear, horror, the
occasional belly laugh.

ANGELINA

It's not really art that makes you despair, Noah, is it?
It's people. It's not that art *can't* make a difference,
it's that you think people *won't*.

NOÈ

You may be right, Angelina. I have spent a long
time with lots of animals. Including the human
animal. When you look at the other species, each
individual animal is usually beautiful in its own way,
each according to its species, as Aristotle once said
to me. Barring acccidents and injuries. Even still
beautiful into old age, often. But look around you,
at any crowd of humans. Almost no-one is beautiful
according to its own species—except, for a while,
children. Michelangelo painted the species as it
might be, should have been, could once have been.
Compare those figures on the Sistine ceiling with
the people looking up at them. But Leonardo saw
humankind as it is, all its deformities, its physical
peculiarities, those wrinkled faces, those misshapen
noses, those sagging cheeks and bleary eyes.
Individuality, if you like. But what makes us
individual is mainly our defects. Few of us match
what a human being is. And it's largely our own
fault, what we do to ourselves, what we do to each
other. And now we are doing it to the whole human
race. The human species is extinguishing itself.

By choice. And idiotically proud of what they are
doing. Like those gladiators, unable to see that they
were simply murdering each other. But at least
those gladiators knew when the end was coming.
These days, people even ignore the volcano.
The fire next time. It's the other animals I feel for.
They will have no ark this time. The planet is their
only ark. And it will burn.

    MARK *(tries to lighten the mood)*
I was feeling quite cheerful when this evening
started!

    NOÈ *(ignores him)*
Of course, those literal-minded christians think it
was all Adam's fault. And Eve's. Well, he was pretty
riddled with guilt. Who wouldn't be? I met him just
the once. Granddad Enoch put me on his knee,
for his blessing. Great Uncle Adam finally died
a few years later. But Auntie Evie was far more
sensible. She knew it wasn't all their fault.
Not just bad parenting. She knew she'd had
a pretty dysfunction-al family, as they call it now,
to bring up. But she also knew you can't blame
the ancestors for your own future.

    ANGELINA *(gently)*
Noè, the story of Adam and Eve is just
another way of trying to make sense of —

    NOÈ *(interrupts)*
And that's another thing! That damn so-called
christian, Boyle, whatever his name was. He said
Job and Jonah and Samson *might* be just *stories*.
And so was I! Well, of course *they* were.
But do *I* look like a *story*!

Mark and Angelina burst out laughing.
After a moment, Noè joins in. And cheers up.

NOÈ

I'm so sorry. I've spoiled the evening for you both.
And you looked so happy together. *(pause)*
Look, I do have things to celebrate too.
My lovely picture of Neemah for a start.
Let's celebrate that properly tomorrow.
Promise me you'll both take the day off tomorrow
and enjoy yourselves. Go and see Rome together.
It's still a beautiful city, with all its deformities,
horrible traffic, planning mistakes, and all the rest.
But do come to dinner with me tomorrow night.
Let me cook a glorious meal for you, all the old
delights I used to love when Neemah was with me.
And she is, in a way, with me again now.
I have her picture, thanks to Mark. *(pause)*
And just maybe she'll hear about the exhibition and
make contact. So I shall cook a proper meal
for you both. And don't worry. It won't be entirely
vegetarian. I love all animals, but a year of hunger
on the ark taught me not to be too sentimental
about them. So long as they were properly treated.
— And I shall even go to bed sober tonight, well,
nearly, for the first time in years. I do have to thank
the Lord, and you, for many things. So do come.

MARK

Yes, we will, Noah. We will. Goodnight.

ANGELINA

Goodnight, Noah, good night. Till tomorrow.

She kisses Noè and he leaves the dining room.
They look at each other.

59 EXT. THE STEPS UP S. ONORIO.
LATE MORNING. SUNNY.

Angelina is nearly at the top of the steep steps. Mark is labouring half way up. A small child races up the steps past him and runs past Angelina. Mark fnally reaches Angelina, gasping for breath.

> MARK
>
> Now I know how the Romans conquered the
> world. They built their city on seven hills,
> then spent a lifetime climbing stairs. By the time
> they were ten, they had leg muscles like elephants.
> And marching to the ends of Europe
> was no problem. March, march, march.

Angelina laughs and pulls him upwards.

60. EXT. BELVEDERE TERRACE.
MORNING. SUNNY.

Mark and Angelina are seated at the small cafe, drinking coffee. It is a beautiful morning.

> MARK
>
> Well, the view was well worth it.
> But, er, where's the gents?

> ANGELINA.
>
> You don't expect me to ask, do you.
> Go and practise your Italian.

In long shot: Mark goes to talk to the man at the counter. He is clearly given complex instructions. Mark looks mildly baffled. But heads off across the road and down the hill.

61. EXT. BELVEDERE TERRACE.
MORNING. SUNNY.

Time has elapsed. Angelina has finished her coffee.
Mark reappears and comes to join her.

> ANGELINA
> What kept you?

> MARK
> It was three hundred yards away!
> In a children's hospital! I couldn't believe
> that was what he was telling me.

> ANGELINA
> But you got it right. Your Italian is improving.

62. EXT. ON BUS No. 115.

Mark and Angelina are seated on the bus together.

63. EXT. PIAZZA SANTA MARIA IN TRASTEVERE.

Angelina is pointing out the mosaics to Mark.
Then they enter the church.

64. INT. SANTA MARIA IN TRASTEVERE.

There is a multiple baptism going on, with several babies
waiting to be baptised, and familes in their Sunday best
filling the main body of the church.

> ANGELINA *(whispers to Mark)*
> Why are there always children and babies around
> when I'm with you, eh?

> MARK
> Because we're in Italy.

65. EXT. PIAZZA SAN CALISTO.

Mark is standing looking at the sign above a busy restaurant across the square.

> MARK
> I like that. We can have some lunch there.
> It says Cafe Socialisto.

> ANGELINA *(laughs)*
> It says Cafe S. Calisto! And the shop next door
> says: 'Shoes for babies and children of all ages. '

66. EXT. VIA PRINCIPE EUGENIO.

Mark and Angelina are standing outside Fassi's gelateria.

> ANGELINA
> Now, don't eat too much ice cream. We're due at
> Noè's for dinner in an hour. But this is one of the
> nicest ways to spend time in Rome.
> Fassi's has been open since Italy began!
> Well, since modern Italy began. 1880.
> Welcome to Il Palazzo del Freddo.

As Mark holds the door open for Angelina,
a sudden stream of thirty to forty children, all dressed for a party,
come down the street and scamper past him, through the door,
which he continues to hold open. Patiently.
Angelina laughs at him.

67. EXT. PIAZZA DI SAN SALVATORE IN LAURO.
EARLY EVENING.

Mark and Angelina are walking hand in hand down a narrow lane.
They turn into the piazza. And stop.

Thick columns of black smoke are rising from Noè's house.
It is obviously severely ablaze.

Several fire engines are in the streets around,
trying to pump water onto the building.

Firemen are trying to break down the heavy door.

Mark and Angelina run towards the building but are stopped
by police and barriers. They watch as the huge house burns.

67. INT. INSPECTOR ZORETTI'S OFFICE.

Mark and Angelina are seated in front of the desk.
Zoretti is silent for a while.

> ZORETTI
> I am truly sorry. *(pause)* There was very little
> anybody could do. The house was like a fortress,
> as I told you, Signor Ferry. All the windows were
> barred. Most were heavily shuttered too.
> And even when the firemen managed to get
> through a window, they found they were just inside
> lots of small rooms, each with a locked door or
> even bars. There were scores of such rooms.
> Even if they got out into a corridor, they found they
> were in a labyrinth. And nobody knew where
> Signor Noè was to be looked for. The fire was so
> intense they had to leave before his body
> could be discovered.

> MARK
> Has anything, anything of him, been found by now?

> ZORETTI
> The building is destroyed. Almost completely.
> Beneath the brick facade the structure was mostly
> wood. It was a huge building, but almost nothing
> remains. We might not even find any bones, ever.

There will be an inquiry, of course. But we will
probably never know what caused the fire to start.
You tell me Signor Noé was going to cook a meal
— perhaps that explains it.

ANGELINA
But you're quite sure it was an acccident.

ZORETTI *(pauses)*
Yes, we're sure. Fairly sure. The blaze seems to
have started inside. *(hesitates)* There was one report
of someone being seen near the house just after the
alarm was raised. And then of a speedboat leaving
the old landing stage on the river just by the house.
But there is actually nothing on the CCTV cameras.
It's the kind of rumour that always starts
in a neighborhood when disasters happen.
We will investigate further, of course, but I doubt
if there is any truth in those rumours. *(pause)*
I assume the house was insured, but we do not yet
know who might benefit. Signor Noè's wife and
children were dead, as I told you. *(pause)*
May I ask, Mr Ferry, if perhaps you still have any
photographs you took inside the house.
Of the house itself. Or any of its contents.
It might help with any insurance claim.

MARK
My photos were all on my laptop. Which I'd left in
the house. That would have been destroyed too.

ZORETTI
That is a pity.

MARK
And was there any sign of, well, art works, statues?

ZORETTI

There were some gold plates and a large gold
candle-stick. Miraculously, they hadn't melted,
even in that incredible heat. But everything else
was just carbon. Will you be staying in Rome
for some time, Mr Ferry?

MARK

Perhaps. I will leave you my contact details.
You will tell us if anything develops?

ZORETTI

Of course. Of course.

They all shake hands. The interview is over.

69. EXT. A YEAR LATER. THE FUNIVIA AT
RAPALLO. SPRING SUNSHINE.

*A large party of very cheerful people, dressed in fine spring clothes,
are queuing to go up on the funivia.*

70. TERRACE OF THE CHURCH
ON MONTALLEGRO.

*As they leave the main door of the church, Angelina, in full bridal
gown, and Mark, in sober wedding suit, are showered with confetti
by a large crowd of friends. They kiss to loud cheers.
The church bells are pealing.*

71. INT. A LARGE ROOM IN THE ALBERGO
ON MONTALLEGRO.

*The wedding guests are noisily enjoying a reception,
with drinks and a buffet.*

*The inn-keeper comes over to Angelina and Mark,
carrying a large brown paper parcel, flat, fairly thin, and rectangular.*

INNKEEPER
Questo è appena arrivato.
Una consegna speciale per voi.

MARK
Grazie, grazie. Ma, da dove? Da chi?

INKEEPER
Non vi è alcun indirizzo. Il corriere dice
che il numero di tracking indica Amsterdam.

MARK *(to Angelina)*
Who do we know in Amsterdam?

*Mark takes the parcel, and looks at it.
Thrre is no visible card or label.*

While Angelina holds it, he carefully unwraps the brown paper.

The guests gradually gather round to watch.

Slowly, a painting is revealed. Mark gasps.

MARK
Good God! It's the *Just Judges* panel
from the Roger Weyden triptych. But—

ANGELINA
And—?

MARK
But that was stolen in 1934! The Nazis searched
for it for years. And everybody else has since.
Good grief!

*Angelina examines the wrapping closely.
Finally she finds a tiny inscription.*

ANGELINA
It says: 'From N & N. With love.'

MARK
Amsterdam! *(suddenly shouts)*
Does anybody know the Dutch
for 'Sign of the Rainbow'?

Fade out?

www.ingramcontent.com/pod-product-compliance
Lightning Source LLC
Chambersburg PA
CBHW070644030426
42337CB00020B/4158